A History of Women's Work

A History of Women's Work

The Evolution of Women's Working Lives

Janet Few

Pen & Sword
HISTORY
AN IMPRINT OF PEN & SWORD BOOKS LTD.
YORKSHIRE – PHILADELPHIA

First published in Great Britain in 2025 by
Pen & Sword History
An imprint of
Pen & Sword Books Ltd
Yorkshire - Philadelphia

Copyright © Janet Few, 2025

ISBN 978 1 03610 526 6

The right of Janet Few to be identified as the Author of this work has been asserted by her in accordance with the Copyright, Designs and Patents Act 1988.

A CIP catalogue record for this book is available from the British Library.

All rights reserved. No part of this book may be reproduced or transmitted in any form or by any means, electronic or mechanical, including photocopying, recording or by any information storage and retrieval system, without permission from the Publisher in writing.

Typeset in INDIA by IMPEC eSolutions
Printed and bound in England by CPI (UK) Ltd.

Pen & Sword Books Limited incorporates the imprints of Archaeology, Atlas, Aviation, Battleground, Digital, Discovery, Family History, Fiction, History, Local, Local History, Maritime, Military, Military Classics, Politics, Select, Transport, True Crime, After the Battle, Air World, Claymore Press, Frontline Publishing, Leo Cooper, Remember When, Seaforth Publishing, The Praetorian Press, Wharncliffe Books, Wharncliffe Local History, Wharncliffe Transport, Wharncliffe True Crime and White Owl.

For a complete list of Pen & Sword titles please contact:

PEN & SWORD BOOKS LIMITED
47 Church Street, Barnsley, South Yorkshire, S70 2AS, England
E-mail: enquiries@pen-and-sword.co.uk
Website: www.pen-and-sword.co.uk

or

PEN AND SWORD BOOKS
1950 Lawrence Rd, Havertown, PA 19083, USA
E-mail: uspen-and-sword@casematepublishers.com
Website: www.penandswordbooks.com

Contents

List of Illustrations		vii
Introduction		xiii
Chapter 1	A Stitch in Time: Clothing the Family	1
Chapter 2	The Canaries: Munitions Workers	6
Chapter 3	Domestic Servants	10
Chapter 4	Over One, Under Two: Straw Plaiting	15
	Anne Stratford's Story	19
Chapter 5	The Match Girls	23
Chapter 6	Fishwives and Herring Girls	27
Chapter 7	The Oldest Profession: Prostitution	31
	Margaret Blackford's Story	39
Chapter 8	Keeping the Family Healthy: Herbal Remedies	45
Chapter 9	The Healing Professions	51
Chapter 10	Feeding the Family	58
Chapter 11	Glove Making	64
	Lilian Norah Guard's Story	68
Chapter 12	The Duties of the Dairy	72
Chapter 13	Cleanliness is Next to Godliness	77
Chapter 14	Pillows, Bobbins and Pins: Lacemaking	82
Chapter 15	Midwifery and Childbirth	86
	Mary Rake's Story	92

Chapter 16	Shopworkers	97
Chapter 17	Women in Wartime: The Land Army	102
Chapter 18	Monday's Wash Day: Laundry Through the Ages	106
Chapter 19	Textile Workers	113
	Ada Fieldhouse's Story	117
Chapter 20	Buttony	120
Chapter 21	Votes for Women: The Fight for Female Suffrage	124
Chapter 22	Teaching and Learning	130
Chapter 23	Pottery Workers	137
	Mary Pankhurst's Story	143

References	149
Selected Further Reading	155
Index	170

List of Illustrations

Chapter 1

Making Clothes at Home © Barbara Watts, used with permission.
Drop Spindle © Janet Few.

Chapter 2

The Munitions Girls by Stanhope Forbes 1918 Wellcome Collection, operated by Wellcome Trust, a global charitable foundation based in the United Kingdom. L0059548 used under Creative Commons Attribution 4.0, from Wikimedia Commons PD-1996.

Chapter 3

La Toilette Raimundo Madrazo, in the public domain from Wikimedia Commons.
Lady's Maid Ironing Lace 1908, Library of Congress, in the public domain from Wikimedia Commons.
The Scullery Maid Jean-Simeon Chardin 1738, in the public domain.

Chapter 4

Plait-School Image George Washington Brownlow, in the public domain.

Chapter 5

Working in a Match Factory 1871 from *The Graphic*, in the public domain from Wikimedia Commons.

Chapter 6

Shucking Oysters in Newhaven Hill & Adamson, in the public domain from Wikimedia Commons.

Chapter 7

A prostitute leading an old man into the bedroom and taking money from him; implying that her services will act like a tonic and preserve his state of health. Coloured etching, 18–, after T. Rowlandson, 1811. Wellcome Collection, operated by Wellcome Trust, a global charitable foundation based in the United Kingdom. L0051171 used under Creative Commons Attribution 4.0, from Wikimedia Commons PD-1996.

Chapter 8

Herb Garden © Janet Few.
An Alembic © Janet Few.
Dandelions © Janet Few.
St. John's Wort © Janet Few.
Dr Williams' Little Pink Pills 1850–1920 Wellcome Collection, operated by Wellcome Trust, a global charitable foundation based in the United Kingdom. L0058211 used under Creative Commons Attribution 4.0, from Wikimedia Commons PD-1996.

Chapter 9

Florence Nightingale from Wikimedia Commons, image in the public domain. Naval nurses and Red Cross train at Chatham. Wounded from Zeebrugge having their wounds dressed. Wellcome Collection, operated by Wellcome Trust, a global charitable foundation based in the United Kingdom. L0009198 used under Creative Commons Attribution 4.0, from Wikimedia Commons PD-1996.

List of Illustrations   ix

Chapter 10

Twentieth-Century Cooking. Image in the public domain, from Wikimedia Commons.
Kitchen at the old King Street Bakery Frederick McCubbin 1884. Image in the public domain from Wikimedia Commons PD-1996.
Hannah Glasse's Complete Art of Cookery Wellcome Collection, operated by Wellcome Trust, a global charitable foundation based in the United Kingdom. L0014987 used under Creative Commons Attribution 4.0, from Wikimedia Commons PD-1996.

Chapter 11

Glove-making *c*.1930s From the Collections of the Library of New South Wales SLNSW15423 used under Creative Commons.
A Collection of Gloves Documentation Centre and Textile museum of Terrassa, used under Creative Commons.

Chapter 12

Plunger or Dasher Churn © Janet Few.
Barrel Churn by Musphot, used under Creative Commons CC BY-SA 3.0, from Wikimedia Commons.
Dairying Apparatus 1904. Creamery Package Manufacturing Company, in the public domain, from Wikimedia Commons.
A Butter Well © Janet Few.

Chapter 13

Sweeping the Floor © Janet Few.
Pewterwort © Janet Few.

Chapter 14

From Goldenberg, Samuel L. *Lace: Its Origin and History* Brentano's (1904) image in the public domain, from Wikimedia Commons.

From Palliser, Mrs Bury, Jourdain, Margaret and Dryden, Alice *The History of Lace* Sampson, Low, Son and Marston (1865) image in the public domain from Wikimedia Commons.

The fireside university of modern invention, discovery, industry and art for home circle study and entertainment John McGovern from a catalogue of 1902 image in the public domain from Wikimedia Commons.

Chapter 15

A woman giving Birth on a Birth Chair. From Eucharius Rößlin, *Der Swangern frawen vnd hebamme(n) roszgarte(n)*. Hagenau: Gran, um 1515. Image in the public domain from Wikimedia Commons.

Chapter 16

*The Confectioners c.*1810 woodcut image in the public domain from Wikimedia Commons.

The Victorian Shop, Morwellham Quay by Robin Drayton, **www.geograph.org.uk/photo/3175985 CC BY-SA 2.0**, used under Creative Commons from Wikimedia Commons.

Chapter 17

Women training to be milkmaids 1917. This image was created and released by the Imperial War Museum on the IWM Non-Commercial Licence. Photographs taken, or artworks created, by a member of the forces during their active service duties are covered by Crown Copyright provisions. Faithful reproductions may be reused under that licence, which is considered expired fifty years after their creation.

Land Girls Audrey Prickett and Betty Long set a rat trap in a hay stack as part of their training on a Sussex farm during 1942. Part of the Ministry of Information Second World War Official Collection, Crown Copyright expired.

Land Girls using a double saw to cut down a tree as part of their training at the Women's Land Army camp in Culford, Suffolk in 1943. Part of the Ministry of Information Second World War Official Collection, Crown Copyright expired.

Chapter 18

Irons © Janet Few.
Drying Clothes © Janet Few.
Washing Board © Janet Few.
Bucket and Laundry Bat © Janet Few.

Chapter 19

Mill Worker created and released by the Imperial War Museum on the IWM Non-Commercial Licence. Lewis G.P., image in the public domain from Wikimedia Commons.
Old Rags into New Cloth: salvage in Britain April 1942. Richard Stone, Imperial War Museum, image in the public domain.

Chapter 20

Dorset Button under construction © Janet Few.

Chapter 21

Suffragette Propaganda left on the Lawn of an English Country House where the Prime Minister, Herbert Asquith, was staying in 1909. Picture Credit: Clovelly Archive and History Group.
WSPU poster by Hilda Dallas 1909, in the public domain, via Wikimedia Commons.

Chapter 22

A Dame School, Thomas George Webster (1800–1886) – N00427. The National Gallery image in the public domain from Wikimedia Commons.

Chapter 23

Pottery in the Making: The work of J. & G. Meakin Pottery, Hanley, Stoke-on-Trent Jack Bryson, Ministry of Information Photographer, 1942, in the public domain from Wikimedia Commons.

Introduction

Women often get overlooked by history. In a patriarchal society, it is the men who spring most readily from the historical record. Men were more likely to make wills, sign leases, join trade guilds, enlist in the armed services, vote and be prominent in local affairs. In the background, women continued to perform numerous unpaid tasks that were vital to both the family unit and the wider community. Many households relied on women to support their husbands in their daily work, without remuneration, be that helping on the family farm, mending fishing nets, or selling the husband's wares. In addition, as a crucial element of the domestic economy, both married and single women often needed to work for financial reward. In order to combine this with childcare and running the home, employment often took the form of home working, on a piece-work basis. Other women sought work outside the home.

Employment opportunities for women were limited by society's attitudes. Firstly, a woman's place was regarded as being in the home; working women might be accused of not paying sufficient attention to their husbands, their children and their household duties. In addition, there was a firmly held belief that education for women was harmful and that there were physiological and emotional differences between the sexes that rendered women unfit for study, or for many roles. Nonetheless, women did undertake a wide range of jobs for which they were paid, although this was, until recently, at a lower rate than the men who were performing the same tasks.

This book outlines three types of women's work: household tasks; home industries; and paid employment outside the home.

It cannot begin to cover every possible role, but the emphasis has been on occupations that involved large numbers of women, or those that shed light on women's employment more widely. This is intended to be an introduction to women's working lives in the various spheres and further reading has been suggested for those who wish to investigate in more depth. Suggestions of resources that can help when researching the various occupations have also been provided.

Some of the chapters include case studies, stories of the lives of women who worked in the particular occupation. It is hoped that this will encourage readers to tell the stories of their own female ancestors and add to the tapestry of women's history.

Janet Few, North Devon, 2025

Chapter 1

A Stitch in Time: Clothing the Family

Today we are used to wardrobes crammed full of clothes, most, if not all, of which have been shop-bought and many of which we may have barely worn. This is a phenomenon of recent generations. Here is a lady recalling the clothing of the post-Second World War period:

> Until the late 1960s, clothes were primarily home-made, if not by the women of the household then by a local dressmaker. Regardless of social class, it seems that garments of this era were minimal in quantity, washed only when visibly dirty and thrown away only when beyond any sort of repair. Adults' clothes would be 'made over' for children and out-grown clothing was passed on to smaller relatives or neighbours. The principle was 'one on, one in the wash and one in the drawer'. Why could you possibly want more than three of anything?[1]

This was the attitude of our ancestors. As in most spheres of life, matters were a little different for the rich but most of our great-grandmothers would have expected to make some, if not all, the clothing for the family. Unless you could afford to employ a tailor, seamstress or dressmaker, ensuring that the family was adequately dressed was an important and time-consuming part of the housewife's duties.

Think for a moment what this would have involved for our ancestresses. If you are imagining them sitting down with a roll of cloth and a needle and thread, this has not always been the case.

Let us consider the woollen clothing: skirts (historically called petticoats); bodices; shawls; breeches for the men of the family; jackets; and hose or stockings. The process began with shearing the family sheep; the one aspect of the task that fell to the men. Don't be fooled into thinking that only farmers had sheep. Even town-dwellers might have a few livestock that would be grazed on their local common.[2] The fleece would need to be washed, perhaps by boiling it up with a plant known, among other things, as soapwort, or bouncing-bet (*Saponaria officinalis*). A wet fleece is incredibly heavy and the housewife would need to dry it. It would be laid on a rack in the sun and turned regularly; this procedure might continue for up to four days before the fleece was thoroughly dry.

Next, the wool needed to be carded, so that the fibres were ready for spinning. This could be done using a teasel, a plant with spiky seed heads, or with carders made from wooden paddles with nails driven through them. The fuller's teasel was preferable to the common teasel but as the name suggests, the common teasel was easier to come by. Fuller's teasels are much harder and more cylindrical in shape, so are better suited to the task. Spinning followed. This might involve using a spinning wheel, or the less-elaborate drop spindle. The advantages of the drop spindle were not just that it was cheaper and easier to produce but with a drop spindle, it is possible to spin on the move and keep an eye on your children or cooking pot at the same time. Drop spindles and basic weaving looms would probably be made at home.

Then came the dyeing process, known as dyeing in the wool. It was also possible to 'dye in the cloth', after the wool had been woven. Dyeing would have been accomplished using plant dyes and many of our poorest ancestors would probably not have bothered with this stage. The yarn was then woven into cloth using a simple wooden frame. The cloth might then be felted so that the warp and weft threads were less obvious. Finally, the needle and thread came into play and the garment could be sewn. Early needles were made of bone or wood, but steel needles and pins were being made in England as early as the seventeenth century.

Knitting[3] was an alternative to weaving, and knitted garments were predominantly stockings or hose, shawls for the women and jumpers for the men. Lack of literacy skills and the costs of printing would mean that it is likely that many of the women worked without knitting patterns, certainly until the mid-nineteenth century. The garments might, nonetheless, be quite elaborate, with distinctive patterns created either by the use of yarn in a variety of colours, or different combinations of stitches. Some patterns are associated with particular parts of the country and traditions were passed down from mother to daughter.

Underneath the woollen garments, home-made shirts or shifts would be worn. In the sixteenth and seventeenth centuries these would almost certainly have been made of linen. In Tudor times, it would be usual for the housewife to spin her own linen from the flax plant but by the 1600s, she would be more likely to be buying in, or bartering for, ready spun and woven linen cloth. Fine linen was more expensive, so was the preserve of the rich, who alternatively might wear silk, or, from the mid-seventeenth century, cotton. The wealthy also set great store by white linen and theirs, at least, would be bleached. A common method of whitening was to soak the linen in urine, as the ammonia acted as a bleach. The linen was then stretched on 'tenterhooks' in the open air to stretch and dry the cloth; the sun would also aid the bleaching process. Those lower down the social scale would probably be content to wear linen that was unbleached, so was grey or beige in colour. By the later eighteenth century, cotton was in use across the ranks of society.

Once you possessed the basic equipment, producing clothing did not require a significant financial outlay. It was, however, hugely expensive in terms of time. The housewife would have to find the opportunity in her very busy schedule to make and mend clothing for the whole family. No wonder many members of working families only possessed one set of woollen clothing, made it last and passed it on when outgrown.

With the coming of the Industrial Revolution in the late eighteenth century, spinning, weaving and knitting became mechanised but most women continued to make clothes at home. The point at which housewives stopped spinning and weaving their own cloth and started buying in bolts of material varied greatly with geography and wealth. Very broadly, you can expect that your seventeenth-century ancestors to have been spinning and weaving woollen cloth for themselves, whereas, by the mid-nineteenth century, this would be less likely. As some parts of the process were outsourced, other skills began to replace them and even our poorer ancestors began to focus on clothing being decorative, rather than merely practical. This meant that, as techniques such as embroidery permeated down the social scale, home-made clothing became more elaborate. The Victorian era brought with it the concept of 'ready to wear' clothing, rather than individually made items for a particular customer. Some women felt that it was a source of pride to make their own garments and that only the inadequate housewife would purchase mass-produced outfits.

By the nineteenth century, sewing machines[4] had started to appear, but these took decades to reach most homes and when they did so, would have been a prized possession. For middle-class women, the nineteenth century saw the rise of the women's magazine, with titles such as *The Englishwoman's Domestic Magazine*.[5] These contained fashion pages and dressmaking tips, as well as giving women aspirations. Increasing literacy also made the use of commercial knitting and sewing patterns more commonplace.

Oral evidence suggests that, at least during times within living memory, women saw the making of the family's clothes as a pleasurable hobby, rather than a chore. It was certainly less arduous than some other aspects of the housewife's role. This blurring of the distinction between work and leisure was commented on by a lady recalling her mother's life in the 1950s:

> Many women seemed to spend their 'leisure' time knitting and sewing. Often this was in order to produce clothing and soft-furnishings for the household, rather than a purely pleasurable activity. My mum's hobbies were also for the benefit of the rest of us, she knitted and sewed and the magazines that she read reflected this.[6]

It is difficult to be sure how our more distant ancestors viewed the prospect of dressmaking. In general, those who left diaries or letters, which might have provided clues, were of the status to employ someone to make clothes for them.

Chapter 2

The Canaries: Munitions Workers

During the First World War, there were over 200 factories in England producing equipment that was required because of the conflict; items such as ammunition, tanks and gas masks. Some of these establishments were built specifically as part of the war effort, others were requisitioned and diverted from their former purpose. The Silvertown factory in London's East End, for example, had previously manufactured soda crystals. The majority of the workers in these factories were female. Although the work of the 'munitionettes', as they were known, is primarily associated with the two world wars, there had been female munitions workers prior to 1914. The 1891 census for Holborn, London, for example, includes several women working in a cartridge factory.

The 'Shell Crisis' of 1915 led to the Munitions of War Act. David Lloyd George, as the newly created Minister of Munitions, had the power to force factories to take on less skilled workers and the number of women in the munitions factories rose fourfold, to approach 1 million. A similar number were to be employed during the Second World War. In 1914, many of these were middle-class girls who wanted to contribute to the war effort. Allegedly, some factories employed a proportion of prostitutes, who had been given the option of munitions work as an alternative to a punishment for soliciting, but this appears to be apocryphal.

By 1917, only 20 per cent of munitions were being produced by men. In theory, a Treasury ruling promised that men and women would receive equal pay and a minimum wage of £1 a week was established. Habitually though, the women may only have been paid at half the rate of their male colleagues. Employers might go to great lengths to ensure that some small part of the role of the male workers was not shared by the women, thus it could be argued that it was not 'equal work' and therefore it did not merit equal pay. Nevertheless, munitions work was comparatively well paid and women were likely to earn more in this way than in other forms of employment open to them. The women were undoubtedly looked down upon and resented by some of their male colleagues, but concessions were sometimes made to the female workforce. For example, on 23 June 1917, *The Nottingham Evening Post* carried a report urging the War Office to provide the women with 'some means of protection, when necessary, from the profane language and swearing of the officials under whom they work'.

During the Second World War, all single women between the ages of 18 and 40 were, by 1942, obliged to do some form of war work, unless they were in essential occupations. The following year, this was extended to those married women who did not have small children. Those who opted for work in munitions factories could be sent anywhere in the country.

Not all the workers in the factories were employed directly in making munitions. On 22 July 1939, *The Leeds Mercury* invited its readers to share memories of the Barnbow factory, in Leeds, during the First World War. Mrs M. Horsfall wrote:

> I was one of the 'fire girls' at Barnbow. … We lived on the premises and had leave of 24 hours every ten days. We had different jobs, such as cleaning and polishing all the fire equipment, replenishing water in the fire buckets, taking the temperature of rooms and opening the windows to keep them at the right temperature. … On night duty we had to patrol the grounds in twos with a punch clock and if we did not fulfill our duties thoroughly, we had our leave stopped, or so many days' pay stopped.

The women worked long shifts of up to twelve hours and the labour was often physically demanding, as they operated the various machines or lifted heavy shell cases. At the height of the war, many of the factories did not close, so night work was required. There were few rest breaks and the job might involve standing up for the entire shift. There were no official health and safety regulations, but the women were provided with overalls, hair coverings and masks, in an attempt to protect them from the fumes. At this time, shoes often had metal nails or heel tips and the sparks that these would generate could cause an explosion, so wooden clogs were worn. For similar reasons, the girls were not allowed to wear jewellery or metal fastenings in their hair.

The result of working with hazardous materials had a significant impact on the women's health and well-being, and several devastating explosions occurred. The full extent of the casualties is difficult to research as, in order to preserve morale, these incidents were not well covered by the press. In 1916, there was an explosion at the Barnbow factory. This was a vast establishment employing 16,000 workers; 35 lost their lives. There was a similar incident at the Silvertown works, when a fire ignited 50 tonnes of TNT and caused a blast that was heard some 60 miles away on the south coast. The explosion left more than 400 injured and 73 dead. Some of the casualties were those who lived in the neighbourhood, or rescue workers. The death toll might have been much higher had the incident occurred earlier in the day, when more workers were in the factory. The Hooley Hill Rubber and Chemical Works, Ashton-under-Lyne suffered a blast in 1917 that killed fifty-six people. This TNT factory was located in a residential area, in close proximity to two gas holders, making the impact of the explosion all the more horrific. In 1918, the National Shell Filling Factory at Chilwell in Nottinghamshire was the scene of the most serious explosion. Here, 250 were injured and 134 died, of whom only 32 could be identified.

Although there is evidence that employers carried out medical inspections and many were concerned for the health of their workers, the long-term effects of working with explosives were poorly understood. The women were nicknamed 'the canaries' because the sulphur turned their skins yellow. Even the babies of women who had been employed in the munitions factories while pregnant had a yellowish tinge to their skin.

Exposure to TNT had serious effects. Although it is thought that there were perhaps 400 deaths from TNT poisoning during the war, many workers suffered for years after the hostilities ceased. The immune system was compromised by prolonged contact with TNT and the women suffered from anaemia and liver failure. Others had fertility problems as a result of their work. Injuries were also caused by the slivers of metal that might run into the women's hands or shear off into their eyes.

Once the war was over, there was no longer such a high demand for munitions and the jobs that were available were given to the men returning from the front. This left many women redundant and not all were content to return to their pre-war roles. Ten days after the Armistice, a female columnist in *The Daily Mirror* lamented the fate of 'the weary munitionettes' and posed the question, 'How are they to fit in to the Reconstruction?'[1] The truth was that, after both the world wars, many found it very difficult to readjust after their time in the munitions factories. Even those who were happy to return to more traditional feminine roles might have to come to terms with having witnessed the death or injury of their colleagues, or find that their own health was impaired. In one form or another, their role as a 'canary' had a life-long effect.

Chapter 3

Domestic Servants

By far the most common form of paid employment for our female ancestors was domestic service. Some would be ladies' maids, cooks or housekeepers in the homes of the gentry, others might be maids-of-all work in a single-servant household, or scullery maids. Many would live-in at their employers' home, others would be 'dailies', living in their own homes. Servants' status rose in line with the social standing of their employer and many would rise through the servants' hierarchy, either by taking a more senior role within the same household, or by a move to a more prestigious establishment.

The census provides details of the numbers involved; in 1851, 10 per cent of the British workforce were servants. The 1891 census showed that 1,386,167 women in England and Wales were in service; more than half of these were between the ages of 15 and 25. Throughout the Victorian period, roughly a third of all women in this age group were domestic servants. Numbers of servants declined sharply after the First World War, when attitudes to female employment changed and labour-saving devices began to take the place of human endeavour. Being a servant not only removed a young girl from her family, so that she was not a drain on the domestic economy, but it was also considered to be an excellent way of gaining the skills that she would need when she became a housewife. It was therefore the obvious employment route for a young, single girl.

Live-in servants were 'all found', in other words they were provided with uniforms, accommodation and food. Wages were therefore not large. In the mid-nineteenth century a live-in cook in a middle-class household might earn £15 a year, with a housemaid earning £11. The hours were long and leisure time was minimal.

The cook and the housekeeper were the senior servants in larger households and were usually older women who would have worked their way up through the ranks. The housekeeper was the intermediary between the mistress and the female servants. She might be responsible for the hiring and firing on behalf of her mistress and would deal with various shopkeepers and tradesmen. She would be expected to order all that was needed for the smooth running of the household, including provisions, fuel, candles and cleaning materials. She would need to be literate, numerate and capable of managing a budget and compiling household accounts. Mrs Beeton's expectations of a Victorian housekeeper were as follows:

> Cleanliness, punctuality, order and method are essential in the character of a good housekeeper. Without the first, no household can be said to be well managed. The second is equally all-important; for those who are under the housekeeper will take their cue from her.[1]

The lady's maid was also held in some esteem and often remained aloof from the other servants. Her tasks would be largely confined to attending her mistress's toilette, helping her to dress and looking after her clothing. She would need to be a skilled seamstress and hairdresser and might well undertake delicate tasks such as the ironing of lace. Mrs Beeton comments:

> Hairdressing is the most important part of the lady's maid's office. If ringlets are worn, remove the curl papers and after thoroughly brushing the back hair both above and below, dress it according to the prevailing fashion. If bandeaux are worn, the hair is thoroughly brushed and frizzed outside

and inside, folding the hair back round the head, brushing it perfectly smooth, giving it a glossy appearance by the use of pomades, or oil, applied by the palm of the hand, smoothing it down with a small brush dipped in bandoline.[2]

Beneath these more senior servants would be a raft of parlour maids, housemaids, laundrymaids, kitchen maids and scullery maids; their titles indicating the areas for which they were responsible. The scullery maid was at the bottom of the hierarchy and rarely left the servants' quarters. She would undertake the roughest work, scouring pots and pans, fetching and carrying for the higher servants and perhaps serving them their meals in the servants' hall. This role was usually that of the youngest girls, in their first position. Hannah Woolley's early eighteenth-century instructions to the scullery maid read as follows:

> Your business is to keep sweet and clean all the several rooms or places, which belong to your charge, as kitchen, pantry, scullery etc. You must wash and scour all the plates and dishes that are used in the kitchen, also the dressers, cupboards, kettles, pots, pans, with all the brass, tin, iron and pewter materials belonging to your kitchen and other apartments. You are to be subservient to and obey the upper cook and the under cook, to make the kitchen fire, bring in sea-coal and charcoal, wind up the jack, take away the ashes and to be ready to perform everything which they shall have occasion to require you to do. You must wash your own laundry and the kitchen linen and when you have made the end of your work fail not to wash and dress yourself rightly and cleanly. And if you are careful and diligent in this place you may be advanced to one more profitable.[3]

Of course, although Woolley's comments are addressed to the scullery maid, it is unlikely that she would be able to read. The manual was for the edification of the housekeeper, whose role was to ensure that the scullery maids who worked under her conformed to these requirements.

Smaller households might employ a cook-general, who would be expected to carry out cleaning tasks as well as cooking. Life would be very different in a single-servant household, where one woman would need to combine all of the roles. In this instance, the lady of the house might well undertake some of the duties. Mrs Beeton says of the maid-of-all-work: 'The general servant, or maid-of-all-work, is perhaps the only one of her class deserving of commiseration: her life is a solitary one and in some places, her work is never done.'[4] After several pages outlining the many duties of the general servant, Mrs Beeton continues:

> A bustling and active girl will always find time to do a little needlework for herself, if she lives with consistent and reasonable people. In the summer evenings she should manage to sit down for two or three hours and for a short time in the afternoon in leisure days. A general servant's duties are so multifarious, that unless she be quick and active, she will not be able to accomplish this. To discharge these various duties properly is a thankless office; but it must be remembered that a good maid-of-all-work will make a good servant in any capacity.[5]

Maids-of-all-work were sometimes called 'slaveys'. In London in the 1880s, The Association for Befriending Young Servants, reported that there were 8,000 such servants in the capital.[6] The association helped young girls to find work, often those who had been discharged from the workhouses, or reformatories. They also provided training and allowed servants to pay for clothing in instalments through their clothing club. The Girls' Friendly Society also provided support for young women in domestic service.

Servants were expected to be invisible, particularly in larger households, freezing if someone entered a room while they were cleaning and using the servants' staircase to avoid contact with those from 'upstairs'. Servants were also anonymous, some were required to change their names to fit with the family's policy of, for example, always having a parlour maid called Mary. Their uniforms helped to ensure that they were regarded collectively and not as individuals.

Although many servants were comparatively well looked after, there were cases of ill-treatment and abuse. Young girls might also be lured to the large towns with promises of domestic work, only to find that they were in thrall to brothel owners. This problem was highlighted by The National Vigilance Association, whose 1899 'Inquiries Concerning Female Labour in the Metropolis', found evidence of this.

For women who did not use domestic service as a stepping-stone to marriage and remained in service, there were difficulties when they became too old or infirm to continue working. Those who were long-term employees might be lucky enough to be awarded a small pension, others would have little option but the workhouse. This was especially likely for live-out or more lowly servants and those who had frequently moved to new employment.

Although the life of a nineteenth-century domestic servant may seem like drudgery by modern standards, many of these women and girls were glad to have employment that was regarded as being less onerous than factory work. Their accommodation might well be better than they were used to at home; they were comparatively well-fed and the work was relatively free from the dangers of some alternative employments.

Chapter 4

Over One, Under Two: Straw Plaiting

Employment opportunities for women were limited by their need to also run the household and look after the children. For this reason, many worked from home in cottage industries that were conducted on a piece-work basis. The usual procedure was for the raw materials to be delivered to the workers' homes each week and the previous week's finished items would be collected and paid for. In the largely rural counties of Buckinghamshire, Bedfordshire and Hertfordshire, the principal home industry was the creation of lengths of plaited straw, which would subsequently be sewn into straw hats. Although there are instances of men being engaged in this work, it was predominantly an occupation for women and girls.

There is evidence for the trade as early as the seventeenth century; straw bonnets are mentioned in Samuel Pepys' diary in the 1660s. In 1689, straw plaiters petitioned in protest against a proposed law that would have required the wearing of woollen hats at certain times of the year. This petition spoke of the 'fourteen thousand persons at least', whose livelihood would be threatened by this measure. Early in the eighteenth century, there were further protests against the importation of plait from the Netherlands.

The chalk soil of the Chiltern Hills, in this area of central southern England, made it easy to grow the strains of wheat straw that were particularly suitable for hat and bonnet manufacture. There was also a plentiful supply of manure for the fields, from the many stables in nearby London. European straw, notably that from Leghorn in Italy, continued to rival the straw grown in England, so the English trade was boosted by the blockades on foreign imports during the French Revolution and Napoleonic wars. In the 1870s, straw hat makers were using cheap Chinese and Japanese plait, making it difficult for the English plaiters to compete. As fashions changed, straw hats were no longer popular and by the twentieth century the trade was reduced to a handful of workers.

Plaiters would be brought supplies of straw by the plaitman and paid by the yard for what they produced; the more complex patterns commanding the highest rate. There were various styles of plaiting, with different levels of complexity. For the simple pattern, the plaiters would chant, 'Over one, under two, pull it tight and that will do'. English Pearl plait was accompanied by the rhyme, 'Criss-cross patch and then a twirl. Twist it back for English Pearl.' A plaiter might finish 60 to 70 yards (approximately 65 metres) of plait each week; it was usually sold in 20-yard lengths.

In common with other home industries, children would be expected to aid in the production process and girls as young as 3 might contribute to the family income by making simple plaits. The centre for the trade was Luton in Bedfordshire and at its peak in the 1870s, over 20,000 women were employed in Bedfordshire alone. In 1851, 4 per cent of the female population of Buckinghamshire were involved in the plait trade, yet, in some villages, the figure was as high as 59 per cent.[1] For these communities, therefore, plaiting might be a source of employment for the majority of the women and some of the men.

In the 1851 census for Aston Clinton, Buckinghamshire, Ann Stratford, whose story is told below, was listed as being a straw plaiter. She was one of 118 females aged between 5 and 25 in Aston Clinton, 59 per cent of whom were working in the plait trade. Often, whole families were involved in straw plaiting. Ann Stratford's father, Richard, was a straw dealer, as was her older brother Peter. Another brother, Henry, was a straw drawer, preparing the straw for plaiting. In 1851, the 239 plait workers in Aston Clinton made up 41 per cent of the workforce in the parish. The vast majority of them were female and under the age of 25.[2]

There were various health problems that arose from straw plaiting. Until the straw splitter came into general use, at the beginning of the nineteenth century, straw was split using a knife, to produce flat strips suitable for plaiting. The use of sharp knives in dark cottages, particularly by young girls, was not a safe activity. The straw had to be wet in order to be manipulated without breaking, so one end was put in the corner of the women's mouths, leading to sores and rotten teeth. Callouses also developed on the thumbs. Sitting hunched over the work was bad for the posture and weaving intricate patterns in poor light was injurious to the eyesight. Plaiting was, however, an improvement on some other cottage industries, as it was also possible to plait standing up, or on the move.

Plait schools were set up where young girls might learn their craft. The girls were crowded together and heating was provided by means of a 'dicky pot', a form of earthenware hot water bottle, containing charcoal or ash instead of water, which was hidden under the skirt. Each girl might have one of these and as they gave off fumes, it created a very unpleasant stuffy atmosphere, which exacerbated chest complaints. In most cases, 'school' was a misnomer as tuition was not given. Instead, the role of the plait mistress was merely to supervise the children as they worked. Parents usually paid 2d a week for a child to attend the school and they also had to supply their daughters' straw. They hoped that the plait mistress would ensure that production was of sufficient quality and quantity to make a profit. Poor-quality plait that could not be sold was known as 'widdle waddle'.

In some cases, children attended a conventional school part-time and plaited for the remainder of the week, but as the height of the plaiting trade was prior to the introduction of compulsory education, more often, plaiting was full-time. The emphasis on plaiting was to the detriment of acquiring domestic skills or undertaking any other form of rudimentary education. The very youngest children would work for seven hours a day, perhaps returning home for a midday meal, but those aged 7 and over might work for another three or four hours each evening. Even when walking to and from the school, children would continue to plait, as the greater the output, the higher the earnings. These schools gained a reputation for being 'places of child exploitation amid exceptional squalor, and even cruelty'.[3]

The 1867 Factory and Workshop Regulation Act made 8 the minimum age for employment in any handcraft industry, of which straw plaiting was one. The same act also regulated the hours for older children. In theory, this did relieve the very youngest children from plaiting in schools, but it was impossible to regulate what was happening within private homes. In addition, a loophole was that the plait mistress could be said to be teaching or supervising her pupils, rather than employing them, therefore the schools were exempt from the legislation.

Plaiting could be a social activity and groups of women would gather outside their cottages to gossip while they plaited. This had the additional advantage that the light was better. The ability for the whole family to plait straw and the fact that, unlike agricultural work, there was no winter slump, meant that plaiting families might be better off than their peers, who had no such home industry to boost the household economy.

An experienced plaiter might bring in a higher weekly wage than her agricultural labouring husband. This meant that many families did not need to seek help from the overseers of the poor, thus keeping the poor rate down, to the delight of the ratepayers. There were, however, suggestions that the women's ability to earn money of their own from plaiting had an adverse effect. Those who worked in the straw plait trade, like those in some other home industries, gained a reputation for immorality. Ecclesiastical

Visitations and Parliamentary Papers of the mid-nineteenth century spoke of prostitution, fornication and the problems of young straw plaiting girls leaving their families at a young age. The girls were also accused of wearing showy clothes, thus attracting the wrong sort of attention. As it was possible to plait while walking, young people were censured for wandering the fields while plaiting in mixed sex groups, which was seen as an invitation to immorality. In 1867/1868, The Royal Commission on the Employment of Children, Young Persons and Women in Agriculture was scathing about the girls engaged in plaiting straw, complaining of their 'great want of chastity'. A number of researchers have investigated levels of illegitimate births to straw plaiters and it seems that there is little evidence that they were significantly more likely to give birth out of wedlock than the general population.

All in all, the opportunity to plait straw gave the women who lived in the counties where it was popular a chance to supplement the household income, to their family's advantage. Our modern sensibilities baulk at the idea of very small children working in this way and indeed the conditions in some of the plait schools were unsavoury. We must remember, however, that if they weren't plaiting straw, these young girls would have been expected to contribute in some other capacity, such as agricultural work, housework, minding younger children, or going into service. So, in the context of the time, those who benefited from an income from plaiting might be in a better position than some of their contemporaries.

Anne Stratford's Story

Ann was the third of the five children of Richard and Grace Stratford née Kingham. She was baptised on 13 May 1834 at Aston Clinton, Buckinghamshire and it seems that she spent the first twenty-one years of her life living there. Many members of the Stratford family were involved in the plaiting and distribution of straw for the hat trade, which centred on Luton. Born on the eve of the Victorian era and dying a year after Edward VII, in 1911, Ann Stratford's life story spans not just the Victorian age but also the rise and demise of the domestic straw plait trade.

At the time of Ann's birth, Buckinghamshire was still suffering from the aftermath of the Swing Riots. In 1830, following an agricultural depression and a series of bad harvests, the plight of agricultural labourers led to protests, during which threshing machines in the south of the country were destroyed under the auspices of the mythical Captain Swing. Conditions and wages were poor, with workers increasingly being hired on short-term contracts and having to find their own accommodation, leaving them destitute when work was scarce. Prior to the Poor Law Amendment Act of 1834, poor relief was inadequate and the obligation of church tithes was punitive. The riots spread across the south of England and were prevalent in Buckinghamshire and the surrounding counties.

The Swing rioters targeted those they perceived as wealthy and overseers of the poor were sent threatening letters, ostensibly from Captain Swing. The rioters demanded increased wages, better conditions, reductions in rents and tithe payments, as well as the destruction of threshing machines. Groups of rioters roamed the countryside damaging threshing machines, burning ricks and attacking property. As labourers in an agricultural community, even if they were not actively involved, the Stratfords must have been affected by the causes and consequences of these troubles.

Before Ann's birth, in 1829, her father Richard, had twice been in court for petty theft. This may have been as a result of the actions of a headstrong young man but the stealing of firewood and turnips suggests perhaps that the family were in dire straits. As poverty tightened its grip, families, such as the Stratfords, were increasingly dependent on income from home industries, in their case straw plaiting. In 1840, Ann's mother, Grace, died of tuberculosis. This left Ann's father, a straw dealer, with three young children, Ann and her two older brothers, to care for.

The plait trade flourished in the years known as the 'hungry forties'. The Stratfords' local plait market would have been 5 miles to the east, in Tring. In 1846, a new market opened up to the west in Aylesbury, 4 miles away from Aston Clinton. The first Aylesbury plait market was held in October and twenty children under the age of 12, from surrounding villages, were give monetary prizes for their plait; one of the winners was 11-year-old Ann Stratford. Mr Thorn of Aston Clinton brought 500 score of plait to sell at this market; the most productive dealer brought 1,300 score and nearly £1,000-worth of plait changed hands.

Ann was recorded as a plaiter in the 1851 census. As mentioned above, she was one of 118 females aged between 5 and 25 in Aston Clinton, 59 per cent of whom were involved in the plait trade. Her father and two brothers were also involved in straw plaiting.

On 13 March 1855, Ann gave birth to an illegitimate daughter, Mary Ann Howe Stratford, in Aston Clinton. There is no DNA evidence to confirm or refute the identity of Mary Ann's father but it seems almost certain that he was William Howe. Ann was to marry William three months later in his home village of Great Kimble, where the couple set up home. What then of the allegation of immorality among plait workers? Ann's eldest brother had been born three months before her parents' marriage. Would Ann, or her mother Grace, have been subjected to the 'rough music' that traditionally accompanied illegitimate births? This involved banging saucepan-lids or tins cans together to cause a commotion outside the mother's home. From this single family's circumstances, it is difficult to draw any conclusions about pre-marital pregnancy, however, in this respect, Ann and her mother were adding weight to the argument of those who reviled the straw plaiting women as being promiscuous.

Ann's husband, William, was an agricultural labourer. Despite the Swing Riots and increased demand for labourers following waves of emigration, agricultural wages were still low in Buckinghamshire in the 1850s. Perhaps attracted by the promise of up to £6 bounty, in 1852, while still a single man, William Howe had responded to a recruiting poster and enlisted in the Royal Bucks King's Own Regiment of militia.

When Ann married William Howe, she was described as a servant of Great Kimble and William was recorded as being a militiaman. It appears that William and Ann spent thirty years living in the same cottage in Great Kimble. According to the 1861 census, Ann was still plaiting. Although no occupation is listed for Ann in the censuses from 1871 to 1891, it is almost certain that she would have continued to plait; women's occupations are notoriously under-represented in the census returns. Toward the end of their lives, William and Ann went to live in Weston Road, in Ann's home parish of Aston Clinton, next to their son Joseph, for a time. They were there in 1891, when, at the age of 60, William was working as a roadman and Ann had lost her hearing. Ten years later, they had returned to Great Kimble and were living in Smokey Row. William was working as a horseman on a farm; Ann was then recorded as plaiting straw. William, described as a farm labourer, died in Great Kimble of exhaustion and acute bronchitis in 1904.

Ann's generation was the last to depend on straw. The market had collapsed in the face of cheap imports and former plaiters were forced to turn to sewing the foreign plait into bonnets, or to seek other means of contributing to the domestic economy. Of Ann's daughters, only the eldest, Mary Ann, took up plaiting, something she did into adulthood, although by the time she was widowed, in 1911, she was engaged in laundry work, there being no longer any demand for plaiting. The remaining daughters went into domestic service, or worked as dressmakers.

On 1 April 1911, Ann died in Saunderton Workhouse infirmary of old age and exhaustion; she was buried with her husband at Great Kimble.

Chapter 5

The Match Girls

You may not have family members who were match girls, you may not have family links to London, but we all have female ancestors. The women who worked in this trade played an important part in a landmark event in women's history and for this reason, their story is included here.

In the 1880s, one of the largest employers of women in the East End of London was Bryant and May's match factory.[1] Initially, Quaker businessmen William Bryant and Francis May imported Swedish matches. Sales rose rapidly, until, by 1860, they were selling nearly 28 million boxes a year. In 1861, they set up a factory in Fairfield Road, Bow in order to produce their own 'safety' matches. The matches may have been safe but the conditions in which they were produced were anything but. By the 1880s, the factory had expanded rapidly and amalgamated with three other match-producing firms. Business was booming as new markets in Asia and Australia were opening up and shareholders' dividends soared. The workers' pay did not reflect the success of the company.

The majority of the 3,000 employees were young women, some as young as 13. This was partly an economy measure but also because their fingers were dexterous. They had to mix the dangerous chemicals, dip the wooden sticks into phosphorus and box the matches. They would work up to fourteen hours a day and were fined heavily for minor transgressions. The match girls were regarded as a boisterous 'rough' group, with flamboyant clothes, frequently sporting large hats with feathers in. In this respect they may not have been very different from their neighbours who worked elsewhere.

The match workers might earn 4–8 shillings a week, depending on their output. Pay was on a piece rate, which meant that, in the interests of speed, the girls became careless with the phosphorus that was a vital ingredient in the manufacture of the matches. White phosphorus was used instead of the safer red form; this was because red phosphorus was more expensive. The mixers, dippers and boxers were exposed to heated fumes. The girls ate their midday meal at the same benches at which they worked, increasing the chances of contamination. This led to phosphorus necrosis or Phossy Jaw, also known as 'the match girls' disease'. The symptoms began as toothache, swollen gums and abscesses. The girls' bones glowed in dark and eventually rotted. This led to open wounds with foul-smelling discharge and eventually to brain damage and death.

The conditions came to the notice of social campaigner and advocate of women's suffrage, Annie Besant. She denounced the trade and its shareholders in an article entitled 'White Slavery in London', in her weekly paper *The Link* in 1888:

> Do you know that girls are used to carrying boxes on their heads until the hair is rubbed off and the young heads are bald at fifteen years of age? Country clergymen with shares in Bryant and May's, draw down on your knee your 15-year-old daughter; pass your hand tenderly over the silky beauty of the black, shining tresses.

This bad publicity put the managers of Bryant and May in an awkward position. They decided to attempt to brazen it out and deny that conditions were so poor. They expected the class system to work in their favour. Their workers were young, female and working class. No one thought that they would dare to face up to their employers. Management also expected support and sympathy from fellow middle-class business owners. Bryant and May tried to force the women to sign a declaration repudiating the article.

In a surprising show of resistance, the girls refused and one was dismissed on a trumped-up charge as retribution. The directors no doubt hoped that this would subdue the remaining women into compliance. To their dismay, 200 girls sought help from Annie Besant, who was able to inspire the workers and co-ordinate a strike. The owners denied that they had tried to pressurise the workers into signing a retraction. Instead, they put the blame firmly on the dismissal of the insubordinate worker, stating that the girl's grievance was that she was being instructed to place the matches in their boxes with heads at alternate ends, instead of all lying in the same direction. This was supposed to reduce the liability to spontaneous ignition but was much slower, therefore drastically reducing the workers' earnings.

Management continued to bluster and threatened to sue Annie Besant for libel. They also planned to use Scottish blacklegs to man the factory and warned workers that they would all lose their jobs, as they would move the factory to Scandinavia. Besant arranged for a group of workers to present their case to parliament. A 15-year-old match girl bared her bald head to an MP and there was a groundswell of support from the middle classes, without which the protest would have failed. Marches and public meetings were organised, with speakers such as Besant herself taking the platform and a fund was set up to support the strikers. Half the employees, some 1,500 workers, took part in the 3-week long strike. By 6 July 1888, the entire factory had stopped work.

The following appeared in *Reynold's Newspaper* of 8 July 1888, suggesting that the directors were still trying to shift the blame. 'Mr Frederick Bryant, the head of the company, has issued a statement, in which he attributes the strike to the interference of professional agitators.' Both the Social Democratic Federation (Britain's first organised, socialist, political party) and The Fenians (Irish Republican activists) were blamed for the strike. Supporters of the Social Democratic Federation were indeed working for the cause of the match girls and their members were encouraged to boycott Bryant and May's products. A number of the workers lived in a predominantly Irish area of East London, hence the association with Irish activists, which is less easy to verify.

After pressure from parliament and public opinion, Bryant finally agreed to bring an end to fines and to provide a separate area for meals in order to reduce contamination. He also agreed that there would be no retribution for strikers and accepted the formation of the newly created Union of Women Match Makers. The campaign to replace white phosphorus with a safer product failed. The Salvation Army opened an alternative match factory using red phosphorus but economics meant that it could not compete. Ironically, it was eventually taken over by Bryant and May. The use of white phosphorous in the manufacture of matches was finally banned in 1908.

Chapter 6

Fishwives and Herring Girls

Most married women worked as unpaid assistants to their husbands in some capacity and the wives of fishermen were no exception. Life as a fisherman's wife was particularly hard. The living was very uncertain, relying on the vagaries of the fish shoals. Fishing was also very dangerous and many fishermen left their wives as widows and their children orphans. Unless the man of the house was only engaged in local, coastal fishing, he might also be away from home for extended periods of time. The nineteenth-century censuses for fishing communities reveal many 'headless' households, where the husband and father was away at sea on census night.

The British trade with the fishing grounds off the coast of Newfoundland is well documented and dates back to the seventeenth century. Fishermen, particularly from the western coasts of Britain, crossed the Atlantic, fishing for cod as they did so. The cod would be dried on the shores of Newfoundland and then sold on, often to European buyers. The wives of those engaged in the Newfoundland trade had to support their families, waiting for several months for their menfolk to return with their wages.

Many fishermen would be working on small family boats and the domestic economy of the fisherman's household was dependant on the contributions of the women. They might be expected to clean and mend nets. The nets would be spread out to dry, debris would be picked off and any holes mended. Many fishermen's wives also cleaned and re-baited fishing lines. Each line might contain over a thousand hooks and fixing small pieces of inferior quality fish to each sharp hook was hazardous.

The women would usually be tasked with preparing the catch, gutting, cleaning, pickling or smoking the fish. Fish was usually salted down in large barrels, with the fishwife placing alternate layers of fish and salt in the wooden barrel until it was full. The fisherman could often not spare the time to sell his produce; that too might be left to his wife, who would walk to market, or go door to door, with her basket of fish, known as a creel, on her back. To supplement their husbands' income, especially if the men were away from home, the women of coastal villages might scour the rocks for mussels, cockles or limpets to sell. In communities that lacked a harbour or jetty, women might wade out to the boat, barefoot, piggy backing their husbands across the shallow water, so that they remained dry, as they began their day's, or night's, work. In addition, when the small fishing boats returned to shore, the women would be on the look-out, waiting to help to winch the boat in across the beach.

Women did not just cure fish that was caught by the family boat. A survey of women's labour, *Toilers in London; or, Inquiries concerning female labour in the metropolis*, published in 1899, wrote of the female workforce in the fish-curing factories of East London:

> Curing fish is largely practised in Stepney. Fish-yards may be found there in which work goes on all the year round, and every day of the week, including Sunday. The fish is fetched from Billingsgate [the major London fish market] to be dried and taken back again when finished. Friday is the best day to see this work, for then the yards are full of fish. These yards are barns, attached to the houses at the back, and covered with tiles or straw. They are generally a few inches deep in water, and the women stand on boxes or stools while preparing the fish. ... All sorts of fish are cured in these places – salmon, herrings, cod, and sprats, but chiefly haddock. The heads of the fish are cut off, the bodies are cleaned and dipped in salt water. They are then strung on iron bars, and hung up to dry.

... The work is very cold in winter. The girls say that icicles often hang from their fingers after they have dipped the fish in the salt water, and that hanging up the fish to dry in the hot cupboards gives them chilblains. ... The usual pay is 2s. 6d. or 3s. a day for the girls and women.[1]

Margaret Ward, in her book *Female Occupations: Women's Employment 1850–1950* refers to a haddock smoking factory in Camberwell, London around the same time. Here the work was non-stop, with the women working day and night shifts to produce 4 tons of smoked haddock a day.

The notorious herring girls were much more independent. Each year, the herring shoals arrived in the Shetland Islands, off the north coast of Scotland, in May or June. The herring then gradually made their way down the east coast of Britain, with the fishing fleets taking advantage of their journey. The season ended in September, by which time the fish were off the coast of the East Anglian ports of Yarmouth and Lowestoft. Herring need to be preserved swiftly, as they do not keep well. This might be achieved by drying, smoking, or salting but the latter was most common. Once salted, the herring were destined for Russia, Scandinavia and Germany and the late nineteenth and early twentieth centuries saw a surge in the demand.

Employers recruited the girls from the east coast ports, offering wages that these women would find attractive. They were paid by the barrel and the best workers could earn up to 10 shillings a day. Several thousand herring girls followed the fleet down the coast every year, in order to gut, clean and pack the fish as it was caught. The women might travel by ship, although some seamen regarded it as unlucky to have women aboard. As the railway network expanded, they might travel by train. The herring girls were predominantly unmarried and the journey south was an opportunity to acquire a husband from another port. In some ports, wooden shelters were erected where small groups of women could live while the fleet was in the area, or they might lodge with local families. The herring girls sometimes brought furnishings with them to make their temporary accommodation more comfortable.

The women worked in teams of three, two gutters to one packer. The herring gutters worked at incredible speeds and the most experienced might maintain a rate of fifty to sixty fish per minute. The gutters also sorted the fish by size and quality. Packing the herring, although requiring immersing the hands in salt, was less hazardous than wielding a razor-sharp gutting knife. The conditions were poor and the days long, perhaps starting as early as 6 a.m. The women were often working outside; the damp and the salt leading to sore hands and chilblains. Oilskin aprons protected their clothing to a certain extent, but it was not a pleasant task. As the packed fish compressed, completed barrels had to be topped up and brine was added before the barrels were sealed.

In common with many groups of women who worked independently, the herring girls acquired a reputation for being brash and riotous. They adopted a distinctive dress, with striped underskirts and a dark flannel overgarment. The women were famed for their knitting whose style often reflected their port of origin. The knitted garments that they produced were an additional source of income.

Both as paid workers and as unpaid assistants to their fishermen husbands, the female workforce was an integral part of the provision of fish for the table and for market.

Chapter 7

The Oldest Profession: Prostitution

Prostitution is often termed the 'oldest profession' and certainly it is one to which many women have turned over the centuries. There is a great deal of difference between the full-time 'professional' courtesan and those at the other end of the scale. There were prostitutes, such as those who became the mistresses of royalty and nobility, who moved in the highest social circles. It was a role that usually came with plenty of fringe benefits. The mistress of the moment would be set up with a household and enjoy a social notoriety, perhaps establishing herself at the head of a rival 'court'. A number of these women were politically astute and wielded considerable power, if only for the duration of their 'reign'. Although their designation as prostitutes might be up for debate, the fact that the likes of Nell Gwynn, Lillie Langtry, Rosamund Clifford (The Fair Rosamund) and Lady Castlemaine are well-known names is a testament to this.

Henry Mayhew, investigating Victorian London, wrote:

> A woman who called herself Lady — met her admirer at a house in Bolton Row that she was in the habit of frequenting. At first sight Lord — became enamoured, and proposed sur le champ, after a little preliminary conversation, that she should live with him. The proposal with equal rapidity and eagerness was accepted, and without further deliberation his lordship took a house for her in one of the terraces overlooking the Regent's Park, allowed her four thousand a year, and came as frequently as he could, to pass his time in her society. She immediately set up a carriage and a stud,

took a box at the opera on the pit tier, and lived, as she very well could, in excellent style.[1]

The story was very different at the other end of the social scale. These women were often driven by poverty. Those left as orphans might take up the 'trade', or be forced to do so, at ages as young as 10. Young girls fetched higher prices, not just because of their youth but because they were less likely to be diseased. It is important to set this in the context of the time. In Britain, the age of consent was raised from 12 to 13 in 1875 and to 16 ten years later. Despite this, girls could legally marry at 12 until as recently as 1929.

Mayhew interviewed several young girls:

My name is Ellen, I have no other. Yes, I sometimes call myself by various names, but rarely keep to one longer than a month or two. I was never baptised that I know of; I don't know much about religion, though I think I know the difference between right and wrong. I certainly think it is wrong to live as I am now doing. I often think of it in secret, and cry over it, but what can I do? I was brought up in the country and allowed to run about with some other children. We were not taught anything, not even to read or write; twice I saw a gentleman who came down to the farm, and he kissed me and told me to be a good girl. Yes, I remember these things very well. I was about eleven the last time he came, and two years after I was sent up to town, carefully dressed and placed in a large drawing-room.[2]

It was not only unmarried women who sold their bodies. It might be a means by which the mother of the family could generate essential extra income. This is almost impossible to identify in the records, as any occupational hazards, in the form of children, would be seen, in the eyes of the law, as the children of the husband. For these women, prostitution was not necessarily a regular activity; many women might boost their earnings, or support their children, by occasionally selling their body. These intermittent prostitutes were often known as 'Dolly-mops'.

There is a school of thought that women in certain trades were more likely to drift into prostitution. Those who claimed to be milliners, manteau makers, dressmakers or laundresses have all been accused of masking their true occupation with a euphemism:[3]

> Fatal experience must convince the public that nine out of ten of the young creatures that are obliged to serve in these shops, are ruined and undone. Take a survey of the common women of the town who take their walks between Charing Cross and Fleet Ditch and I am persuaded more than one half of them have been bred milliners, have been debauched in their houses and are obliged to throw themselves upon the town for want of bread.[4]

In 1783, parents were cautioned against apprenticing their daughters to the dressmaking trades, which were regarded as being 'actually seminaries of prostitution'.[5] Of course, thousands of women genuinely followed these trades. Dressmakers, for example, might have clothes that would attract attention and they would seem to have more opportunity to meet potential clients than a live-in housemaid. Perhaps this is how the association has arisen.

In 1789, *The Kentish Gazette* reported:

> Sir William Dolben informed the House that he intended to move for leave to bring in a Bill to prevent Prostitutes from infecting the streets. The general titter which prevailed in the House, made it impossible for those in the gallery to hear distinctly what fell from the Hon. Baronet on the subject.[6]

This is in sharp contrast to an opinion expressed in *The Norfolk Chronicle* three years earlier. This article quoted the figure of 50,000 London prostitutes, of whom 10 per cent died annually. It went on to say:

> There are those who maintain that female prostitutes are necessary to good order, and they argue from the necessity that a few should be sacrificed for the good of the community at large. If there were not prostitutes and brothels, say they, no man's house would be sacred from the violation of lust and brutality ... Prostitutes have very improperly been stiled [sic] women of pleasure; they are women of pain, of sorrow, of grief, of bitter and continual repentance, without a hope of obtaining pardon, cut off from society, they become desperate. Yet let it be remembered, that he whose example should be followed by Christians, has shewn that their sins are to be forgiven.[7]

Somewhere in between the Dolly-mop and the courtesan were women for whom prostitution was their only source of income. They frequently worked for a pimp or 'Madam' who, in return for a sizeable slice of the earnings, might provide a room and some degree of protection. The money that the women could earn varied widely but was frequently far more than they might receive as servants or seamstresses. A well-to-do prostitute might charge £10 per customer, whereas her poorer sister could still ask 10 shillings. At the end of their careers, the old and the diseased would attempt to bring in a few pence by obliging the less discerning, and the London parks were notorious for this kind of encounter. As early as the 1780s, London mayor Sir John Fielding called Covent Garden 'the great square of Venus'.

Women who engaged in prostitution, on a regular or occasional basis, were vilified; however, the attitude towards their clients was very different. Men who used the services of a prostitute were regarded benignly and were provided with guides to the whereabouts of brothels. Reinforcing the opinion of Sir John Fielding, was the publication *Harris's List of Covent Garden Ladies*, produced annually from 1757–1795. This listed the woman's age, appearance and accomplishments, such as singing and dancing. In addition, the reader was informed of the 'specialities' of her trade, her address and the price, which ranged from 5 shillings to £5. Produced in the 1830s and 1840s, a similar aid to those seeking the services of a London prostitute was *Swell's Night Guide to the Bowers of Venus*, which identified brothels and places frequented by prostitutes.

Although brothels were discouraged and at times outlawed, many worked from a 'bawdy house'. There is an entry in the 1841 census return for Lambeth, where the enumerator has written:

> The houses in Jane Place are occupied principally by prostitutes who denied to the enumerator that any male had slept therein in Sunday night the sixth instant. However, upon careful enquiry among the neighbours he the said Enumerator ascertained that not less than twelve or fourteen males whose ages varied from 20 to 50 years had aboded in the said Jane Place on the night of the 6th instant.

Estimates of the numbers involved in prostitution vary widely. In the mid-nineteenth century, the City Police, reporting to Dr Ryan, estimated that there were 7,000–8,000 in London; whereas the Bishop of Exeter and Henry Mayhew came up with a figure that was ten times that number. Attitudes to prostitution varied, with some condemning it outright. The increasingly vocal lower classes, following the French Revolution, were often blamed for the rise in prostitution. By the nineteenth century, this was seen to be a problem that required some form of official control. In 1802,

William Wilberforce presided over The Society for the Suppression of Vice, which acted against a variety of 'ills', from snuff-taking to blasphemy. In 1835, The London Society for the Protection of Young Females, and Prevention of Juvenile Prostitution was formed. The Vagrancy Act of 1839 reinforced that of fifteen years earlier and outlawed 'loitering for the purposes of prostitution or solicitation, to the annoyance of passengers or inhabitants'.

Despite Mayhew's estimate that there were 80,000 prostitutes in London in the mid-nineteenth century, the 1861 census for the whole of England and Wales lists just 683 individuals whose stated occupation was that of a prostitute. It would, of course, be unusual for a woman to self-identify in this way. Many thousands would be disguised as laundresses, dressmakers and domestic servants. There are exceptions, but it is usually those in institutions who are labelled as prostitutes by the authorities and therefore appear as such in the censuses.

There were obvious links between prostitution and other forms of crime. Sometimes the prostitute was used to distract the client, in order to enable an accomplice to commit a robbery. Prostitutes were frequently in the courts for 'overlaying' an illegitimate child, an offence that seemed to be viewed much less seriously than other forms of murder.

With prostitution inevitably comes sexually transmitted disease and this became a particular problem among the armed forces, with large numbers of women frequenting the areas surrounding army barracks and naval dockyards in order to dispense sexual favours. Service records often note incidences of venereal disease. In a draconian attempt to control this, the Contagious Diseases Act was passed in the 1864. Initially, this gave the police the right to arrest women found near barracks, or in ports in certain towns, but the jurisdiction was later extended, so, by 1869, it covered a wider area; women could also be apprehended within a 15-mile radius of the towns covered by the acts.

The apprehended women, who might include respectable passers-by, were subjected to compulsory examination and those infected were forcibly hospitalised in 'Lock Hospitals', or, if these were full, in workhouse infirmaries, for anything from three months to a year. In 1869, the minimum period was extended to six months. There were many protests against these measures, particularly as there were no checks on the male clients. The women's suffrage movement took up the cause and the acts were finally repealed in 1886, primarily due to the efforts of social reformer, Josephine Butler.

Josephine Butler had been largely responsible for the raising of the age of consent. While conducting her campaign to have the Contagious Diseases Acts repealed, she was appalled by how young some of the girls were. Together with William Thomas Stead, the editor of *The Pall Mall Gazette*, she set out to expose the scandal of child prostitution. Stead purchased a 13-year-old girl from her mother for £5 and the subsequent outcry led to the 1885 Criminal Law Amendment Act, raising the age of consent from 13 to 16 and brought in measures to prevent child prostitution. It became illegal to procure a girl under the age of 18 for the purposes of prostitution; obtaining a prostitute by intimidation, fraud or the administering of drugs was also outlawed.

London's prostitutes and their way of life were under public scrutiny during the reign of Jack the Ripper in the 1880s. It is not to be suggested though that prostitution was a London phenomenon, or an exclusively urban one. Most genealogists have come across the local 'friendly' ladies in their research; those who bear several illegitimate children, sometimes finally marrying and leading a more conventional life. They were common in the country villages and were perhaps more likely to be identified, as it was difficult to remain anonymous in a small community. They might then find themselves in front of the courts for fornication or adultery. A witness at the ecclesiastical court in Barnstaple, Devon reported in 1572:

> This deponent having occasion to go to a lane against Chapel Cleve Weir by chance he found one John Grene lying upon Catherine Clotworthie in the snow in the same lane and his hose down and her clothes up but otherwise he hath reported of her except this respondent hath also said that he heard Richard Thomas say that she the said Catherine was a whore. [Spelling has been modernised.]

Those who were found guilty of sexual offences in the ecclesiastical courts would usually have to perform a public act of penance. The resulting records reveal the attitudes towards any form of sexual transgression. Philip Buckingham and his wife, Elizabeth, of Northill in Cornwall, did marry and there is no suggestion that Elizabeth was a prostitute, but, in 1760, were still found guilty of fornication, as the birth of a child showed that they had pre-empted the ceremony. A document from the court sets out their punishment:

> Whereas you have been prosecuted in the Archdeaconry Court of Cornwall for the crime of fornication each with other before your intermarriage and whereas the said crime being objected to you, you have confessed the same and submitted yourselves to the censure of the said court, you are therefore enjoyned and required by the authority of the worshipfull John Sleech, clerk, master of arts, archdeacon of the Archdeaconry of Cornwall, lawfully constituted to do and performe the penance following (that is to say) That you shall on the next Sunday after the receipt thereof in the afternoon immediately after Divine Service in the Chancell of the Parish Church of Northill abovesaid say and repeat the words following (to witt) we Philip Buckingham and Elizabeth Buckingham do humbly confess and acknowledge that we have highly offended Almighty God by committing the foul sin of fornication each with other before our marriage,

for which we do here in your presence declare our hearty sorrow and penitence and promise (by God's assistance) amendment of life for the future, beseeching God to pardon us and desiring you to pray. And thereupon you are to say and repeat the Lord's Prayer upon your knees.

Just thirty-four years earlier, the same court had demanded that penitents should be bare headed, bare legged, with a white sheet over their shoulders and a white rod in their hand, while begging forgiveness.

Some sought to reform the women and set them on a new path. As early as 1751, *The Scots Magazine* was writing of the 'many noble charities' in Edinburgh whose aim was the 'support of repentant prostitutes'. The Magdalene Hospital for the Reception of Penitent Prostitutes was set up in 1758 in London and the girls were put to laundry work. This was the first of a worldwide series of similar homes. The appalling conditions in the Magdalene Laundries, particularly those run by the Catholic Church in Ireland, are now notorious. In 1829, The British Penitent Female Refuge opened in Bethnal Green, London, 'to restore guilty females to the paths of virtue'. The author, Charles Dickens, was a well-known reformer and set up Urania Cottage, with the aim of rehabilitating 'fallen women' and sending them to the colonies. Prime Minister William Gladstone, was another prominent figure who conducted a campaign in order to rehabilitate prostitutes.

At a time when poverty was rife, it is easy to understand why some of our desperate female ancestors might resort to prostitution, thus putting their health at risk and earning the disapproval of their neighbours.

Margaret Blackford's Story

Please note that this case study includes an account of a child murder, which some readers may find distressing.

In April 1907, 27-year-old Henri Berney, a Swiss chef, was charged with demanding £1 with menaces from a barman, Sidney Harbord. Henri's co-accused was Margaret Blackford, a 23-year-old woman who was co-habiting with Henri, posing as his wife. The case against Margaret was discharged as she gave evidence against Henri, saying that he had coerced her into prostitution. Henri was then charged with living off Margaret's immoral earnings, as well as threatening both Harbord and the arresting officer with a revolver. Henri said very little to defend himself against the charge of living off immoral earnings but commented that they were poverty-stricken, as he was out of work. He was sentenced to three months in prison with hard labour, with the recommendation that he be deported on completion of his sentence.

Margaret's was a sad case of a woman being forced into selling her body by the man she was living with. Her life, up until she met Henri, reveals nothing that might hint at her unfortunate future. She was born in 1883, in Cranbrooke, Kent, the eleventh of twelve children of Mark and Hannah Blackford. In 1891, Margaret was living with her parents, six older brothers and a younger sister, in a four-roomed cottage in Benenden, Kent, where her father worked as an agricultural labourer. Three older sisters had already left home and one had died in infancy. Margaret was baptised on 29 July 1883 at St George's, Benenden.

Despite being part of such a large family, who must have been living in relative poverty, Margaret seems to have benefited from compulsory education and the opening up of new employment opportunities for women. She was taken on as an assistant at a large draper's store in Croydon, over 40 miles from where she was born. Perhaps she had spotted an appeal for staff in a local newspaper. Croydon was a bustling, rapidly expanding town on the southern outskirts of London and the store was a branch of the prestigious Bourne and Hollingsworth's in Oxford Street. The establishment occupied a prominent place on Croydon's High

Street. The five-storey building has an impressive façade and no doubt Margaret and the other assistants lived in the upper floors of the building. This was a far cry from Margaret's upbringing in rural Kent. Although being a shopworker was regarded as a respectable occupation, conditions were notoriously poor, as Chapter 16 shows. Within two years, Margaret had returned to Kent and was making good use of her education, being employed as a bookkeeper in a Margate hotel.

While working in Margate, she became enamoured of the hotel's French-speaking, Swiss chef Henri Berney. The couple began an intimate relationship that was to have consequences that went far beyond Margaret being forced into prostitution. In September 1903, Margaret and Henri, posing as husband and wife, left for London. Margaret became pregnant and in July 1904, Blanche Marguerite Berney was born. Her birth was registered as both Berney and Blackford.

Had Margaret's experiences of being one of a very large family made her wary of motherhood? It transpired that she was keen avoid to breastfeeding. Maybe it was Henri who did not want the inconvenience of a child; perhaps both parents needed to be free to work. For whatever reason, Blanche was put out to nurse in Eastbourne, nearly 80 miles away on the south coast. There seems no logical reason for choosing to place the baby at such a distance. Henri paid for the support of the child for over a year but then the foster family assumed responsibility and Blanche disappears from the records. There was no formal adoption at this time but perhaps her foster family changed her name, meaning that she cannot now be identified.

In November 1905, Margaret and Henri had another child, Cyril, who was also put out to nurse, this time in Crowhurst, not far from his sister. Cyril was baptised in Crowhurst in the summer of 1906, but Henri and Margaret were, at that time, living in Brixton, south London. Cyril can be found in the 1911 census as a 'nurse child' of the Goodsell family in Crowhurst. He never returned to his birth family and remained in the Crowhurst area for the rest of his life.

By September 1906, Henri and Margaret were on the move again. Now out of work, they were living at 10 Liverpool Street, King's Cross and Margaret was expecting their third child. Despite this, when their savings ran out in the November, Henri sent Margaret, who was by then more than six months pregnant, out on to the streets to bring in money. At 7 a.m. on 7 January 1907, attended by a fellow lodger, Mrs Woodward, Margaret gave birth to a boy, whom she named Reginald. Margaret believed that the baby was two weeks early and perhaps the birth did not go well, as Henri wanted her to go to the French Hospital. Margaret resisted because she knew, if she took the baby with her, she would be expected to breastfeed, which she was not willing to do. She claimed that, after her daughter was born, the doctor had advised her against breastfeeding.

Henri was determined that this child too should be sent away and consulted *Dalton's Weekly*, looking for advertisements for those who would take a nurse child. Allegedly, Henri said that he did not care what became of the child as long as it went away. He then told Margaret that he would take the baby to Waterloo, to be looked after by a Mrs Robinson, who was nursing Henri's brother's child. The doctor visited and agreed to take Margaret into the French Hospital if the baby was catered for. Henri's sister-in-law, Victoriana, called and the baby was washed and dressed in clothing that Mrs Woodward had bought with money that Margaret had borrowed. The last Margaret saw of Reginald was when Henri and Victoriana left with him. After ten days in hospital, Margaret returned to 10 Liverpool Street and to Henri, who said that Reginald had been taken to the country. Believing her son to be alive and well, Margaret registered the birth on 1 February.

Henri and Margaret moved three times in the next six weeks, at which point Margaret questioned Henri as to Reginald's whereabouts. Initially, Henri said, 'Never you mind, you won't see him again; he is in the Thames,' but he almost immediately denied this. Margaret was obviously not convinced as she resolved to take matters further, at which point Henri said, 'If you dare give me away, or say a word, your life is not safe,' so Margaret did not pursue this and was soon back on the streets. It was at this juncture that Henri and Margaret found themselves in court.

As a result of the accusation of demanding money with menaces from Sidney Harbord, Margaret gave evidence to the police. They presumably investigated further and on 28 May 1907, Henri Augustus Berney, describing himself as an electrician, was found guilty of the murder of Reginald Berney and consequently sentenced to death. On 14 February, the body of a baby had been pulled from the Thames. The inquest determined that the infant had been in the water for fourteen or fifteen days, so it may be that Reginald was already dead when Margaret registered his birth.

The trial revealed that while Henri was living with Margaret he was often absent from home, working in hotels in Birmingham, Harrogate and Cromer, as well as making two journeys to Australia with P and O liners, working as a chef. Margaret had tried to find the address of Mrs Robinson, where the child had allegedly been taken but Henri wouldn't tell her and Victoriana stated that she didn't know, despite her own child being cared for there.

Henri tried to claim that the child had stopped breathing before he put the body in the Thames but this was not believed by the jury. His death sentence was later commuted to life imprisonment and having spent time in Pentonville Prison and at Portland in Dorset, Henri was extradited in 1917. It seems he may have later gained his freedom as there is a record of a Henri A. Berney of the right age, describing himself as an engineer, travelling from Malaysia to Lausanne, via London, in 1947.

Margaret remained in London and in 1921 was living at 56 Victoria Mansions, South Lambeth Road with her 11-year-old 'niece' Phyllis. Margaret was described as an out of work blouse maker. Further investigation reveals that Phyllis was in fact Margaret's daughter. Phyllis was born in Tooting on 7 September 1909 but was baptised on 11 July 1917 at St Mark's Lambeth as the daughter of Margaret Blackford. Her address was given as Belgrave Hospital, 198 Brixton Hill. Other entries are also marked Belgrave Hospital but with different addresses, suggesting that Phyllis was in hospital but that Brixton Hill was her home address. Phyllis never married and died in Lambeth in her eighties. There are no clues to the identity of her father.

Margaret died in 1938. She and Phyllis were living at 10 Cedars Road, Clapham at the time and Margaret had returned to her work as a bookkeeper. They had been to the dog races at Wembley and were crossing the road at Hyde Park Corner about 11.20 p.m. when Margaret was hit by a car and died of her injuries. The car was estimated to be going at 40–45mph but the traffic lights were green and the pair had crossed despite this. The death was deemed to be an accident. By strange coincidence, the driver of the car was 18-year-old Leonard Berney, a caterer. Interestingly, Leonard had been fined for dangerous driving the previous year, when he was still at school. Leonard was no relation to Henri, his name had been anglicised from a Germanic name, perhaps due to relations with Germany in the 1930s.

Chapter 8

Keeping the Family Healthy: Herbal Remedies

For our ancestors, a visit to a medical professional was an expensive business and would only be resorted to in extreme cases. The women of the household would be expected to treat most family ailments and injuries. This was frequently accomplished by means of herbal potions. The medicinal use of plants goes back to ancient times, with Babylonian tablets from 3,000 BCE describing herbal remedies. Some of these 'cures' are weird and wonderful in the extreme, prompting those with twenty-first-century medical knowledge to wonder if they could possibly have worked. Of course, even today, a large part of the world's population relies on plant-based medicines, many of which are known to be beneficial. Initially, the use of herbs would have been on a trial and error basis. If they were not seen to help, then the experiment would be unlikely to be repeated, would not be recorded and would not be passed on. For this reason, it must be concluded that the cures that appear in herbals, or books of household management, for example, must have been seen to work. Why they worked is a different matter. In some cases, there would have been scientific benefits, in others, the medicines had a psychological, or placebo, effect.

For our female ancestors, there were problems associated with administering herbal remedies. Firstly, the woman needed to know which herb was appropriate for a particular ailment and also what part of the herb to use. Roots, berries, flowers, leaves, seeds and bark might all be employed. Many households kept private books of 'Receipts', or recipes for cures. Some found their way into print.

The most famous herbals of the seventeenth century were those by Nicholas Culpeper and John Gerard, both of which are still available in facsimile form. The difficulty was that many seventeenth- and eighteenth-century women were not literate, so printed herbals were of little use. The information they needed would have to be learned from their mothers, remembered and passed down through the generations.

The next obstacle was accessing the required herbs in an era when growing seasons were short. It was acknowledged that the herbs were most effective if used fresh, but it was clearly not always possible to gather fresh herbs, especially in the depths of winter. This meant that the plants had to be collected when they were available and preserved in some way for use throughout the year. There were a variety of methods by which this could be done. Some herbs were suitable for drying. The word 'drug' comes from the Old Dutch for 'to dry'. The plants would be placed in the bread oven as it began to cool, hung from the rafters near the fire, or laid in hot sun to accomplish this. Other herbs would be mixed with a little animal fat to make a pill. It was possible to distil herbs using an alembic, or helm, or to turn them into a salve by mixing the plant material with beeswax.

There were several ways of administering herbs. They could be taken orally, rubbed in, or given in the form of an enema. Decoctions were made by boiling herbs in water, or the herbs could be infused by adding already boiling water to make a medicinal tea. Poultices were fashioned by mixing herbs with flour paste, barley or suet, which was then spread on a cloth. Plaisters, an early form of plaster, involved putting the herbs into liquid fat and allowing it to harden. When it was required, the fat was melted and rubbed on a cloth, which could then be applied. Comfrey roots were commonly used in plaisters that would be utilised in instances of broken bones. For this reason, comfrey was also known as 'knit-bone'.

Some of the recipes recommended by the herbalists were not straightforward. Hannah Woolley's cure for plague required 1lb of each of the following: rue; rosemary; sage; sorrel; celandine; mugwort; the tops of red brambles; pimpernel; wild dragon; agrimony; balsam; and angelica. Apart from the difficulty of gathering such a range of plants, just imagine the sheer quantity required to constitute 1lb of scarlet pimpernel, a tiny, red, ground-covering plant. This illustrates that being the family herbalist was not an easy task.

So what were some of these remedies that our great-grandmothers might have used? Here are just a few from the seventeenth to the twentieth centuries. It is interesting to note that many recommendations from the 1600s were still being used in the 1900s. Hannah Woolley's plague remedy has already been mentioned, but for those who found her recipe daunting, there were other methods that were used in an attempt to cure those suffering from this deadly epidemic. Less complex herbal options included mixing rue with honey and egg yolk and using it as an ointment. Alternatively, one might urinate on a mixture of yarrow, tansy and feverfew and get the patient to drink the strained liquid. If these failed then you could always follow a common plague recipe that required powdered unicorn horn[1] and frogs' legs. In addition, the plague boils could be covered in chicken feathers or a dead pigeon or toad.

Turning to other complaints, a book of Receipts from 1680[2] suggests that the following is 'An Excellent and approved Medicine for the Collick and stone':

Take the little round knobbs that are upon the fish called the Thornback, whereupon the prickles doe grow, and wash them cleane being well boyled drie them in an oven, untill you can beate them to powder, when they are very finely beaten, take as much as will laye upon a groat and scrape them also take of the whitest egge shells cleane washed & dryed & finely powdered the same quantity as of the other powder mixe them together & put them into a spoonfill of white wine

& drinke a good drauft of white wine after it about an houer after you have taken it drinke a cup full of broth make of mutton or Veale, wherein is boyled a good handful of garden parsley. You may beate with the powder a little white sugar candy and one clove or two at the most to give it a good taste. You may take the powder as often as you see occasion, you must use moderate exercise after.

This is all very well but a number of the suggested ingredients would not be available to the average housewife, plus and wine, sugar and cloves all came at a cost. What most of our ancestors needed were remedies that required the use of plants that they grew in their own herb gardens.

Dandelions were used for urinary complaints, which may have given rise to its nickname 'pis-a-bed'. Feverfew was administered for headaches and fennel for indigestion. Those who suffered from arthritis were encouraged to beat themselves with stinging nettles. Lavender water would be applied to the temples in cases of migraine and rosemary was though to aid the memory and, as such, was also used as a symbol of remembrance: 'Rosemary for Remembrance'. Mental illness was not neglected. St John's Wort was given for depression and those diagnosed with lunacy wore a hessian sack containing buttercups round their neck. Gerard states that borage flowers and leaves 'put in to wine make men and women glad and merry, driving away all sadness, dulnesse and melancholy'. It is debatable how much of this was due to the borage and how much to the wine.

A number of herbs were used to end an unwanted pregnancy, including cuckoo-pint. The berries of the cuckoo-pint were also mixed with hot ox dung and spread on bread as a cure for gout. Fortunately, this appears to have been applied as a poultice, rather than eaten! Dung and urine were of course free and often feature in cures. Powdered peacock dung was recommended for epilepsy, although obtaining it might have posed a problem for our ancestresses.

It is not generally known that John Wesley, founder of Methodism, also gave advice on 'easy and natural methods of curing most diseases'. His book *Primitive Physic* was first published in 1770. Interestingly, he annotates a number of his suggestions with the word 'tried'. His many and varied cures for asthma include living for a fortnight on boiled carrots only; 10 to 60 drops of Elixr of Vitriol in water three or four times a day, or taking 8 to 10 grains of finely beaten saffron, nightly. For hoarseness, Wesley instructs the patient to rub the soles of the feet with garlic and lard before the fire.

By the time *Mrs Beeton's Book of Household Management* was published in 1861, various patent medicines were available for purchase and a number of her recommendations involve mixing commercially purchased ingredients with those that the housewife could gather for herself. She advocated making a general-purpose lotion comprised of a dessertspoonful of Goulard's extract and 2 tablespoonfuls of vinegar in a pint of water, or, as an alternative, ½oz of sal-ammoniac, 2 tablespoonfuls of vinegar, 2 tablespoonfuls of gin or whiskey and ½pt of water. For lumbago, Mrs Beeton suggested 1oz of camphor in a pint of rectified spirits of wine, into which 4oz of hard white soap was to be dissolved, mixed with 4oz of rosemary oil. *The English Woman's Domestic Magazine* of a similar era and edited by the Beetons, recommended soaking ivy leaves in vinegar and applying them to corns.

Nineteenth-century newspaper adverts extol the virtues of numerous connections, many of dubious provenance. The claims for some of these products were effusive. One of the most well known was Dr Williams' Little Pink Pills for Pale People, which claimed to cure locomotor ataxia (a symptom of, among other things, syphilis), partial paralyxia, seistica, neuralgia, rheumatism, nervous headache, the after-effects of la grippe (influenza), palpitation of the heart, pale and sallow complexions and all forms of weakness in male or female. As such medicines became more affordable, there was less reliance on the housewife to produce her own. The use of home-made medicines did, however, continue and it is likely that they were more effective than many of the 'quack' remedies that were sold.

Even our more recent ancestors devised home-made cures. Women writing of medicines in the period after the Second World War recalled the following: vinegar for wasp stings; soaking chilblains in urine; a dose of liquid paraffin or soap pellets up the rectum for constipation; cloves for toothache; goose grease on the chest for colds; and honey and lemon for coughs.[3]

Keeping the family healthy was just one of the many and varied tasks of the housewife of the past. It required skill and effort and was taken very seriously.

Chapter 9

The Healing Professions

Unqualified nursing began in the home and as we have seen in the previous chapter, housewives were expected to provide nursing care for their families and servants. The development of this into a respected profession, with a formal qualification structure, has been comparatively recent. The exclusion of women from professions arose primarily from the firmly held belief that women were physiologically and emotionally unsuited to education and that it would be detrimental to their health. In the case of medicine, there was the additional obstacle that it was considered unthinkable that respectable women should come into contact with bodily fluids and unclothed male bodies.

Until the middle of the nineteenth century, nursing was considered to be a lowly occupation that required no training and seemed to attract those of very little ability. Florence Nightingale referred to these 'nurses' as being 'too old, too weak, too drunken, too stolid or too bad to do anything else'.[1] Although there were a few earlier attempts to improve hospital conditions, it was not until the activities of Florence Nightingale and Mary Seacole, during the Crimean War of the 1850s, that nursing became a well-regarded profession.

Florence Nightingale continued to make efforts to ensure that the state of hospitals improved and that nursing care was of a high standard. Her ideas and books were used well into the twentieth century. The Florence Nightingale Museum **www.florence-nightingale.co.uk** is housed at London's St Thomas' Hospital. Its website contains useful background information about the history of nursing and Florence's life. The London Archives houses the

Nightingale Collection, with many useful documents. The National Archives (TNA) holds bundles of correspondence, applications and recommendations for those who wanted to nurse in the Crimean War. Sidney Herbert's notebook, giving details of nurses appointed to serve in that war, is held at the Wiltshire and Swindon History Centre. Those recruited were often middle-class young women, such as Florence herself.

By the 1880s, training was available and usually took place within the hospitals. The Hospital Records' Database may help to locate the records for a specific hospital www.nationalarchives.gov.uk/hospitalrecords/. For example, records of the nurses who trained at Guy's Hospital and the Nightingale Training School, in London, are at the London Archives. The British Nursing Association and the Nightingale Fund, also provided training. *Burdett's Hospital Annual* (later *Burdett's Hospital and Charities Annual*), issued annually from 1890–1932, is another way that you may identify hospitals and other institutions that could have employed doctors or nurses. Some twentieth-century editions are available via Ancestry www.ancestry.co.uk. Burdett's also produced an *Official Nursing Directory* between 1894 and 1903. The 1898–9 edition is on Ancestry.

The length of a nurse's training period, pay and conditions varied from institution to institution. Those who were further up the social scale, such as the daughters of the professional classes, were often exempt from parts of the training and might not be expected to carry out the most menial and unpleasant tasks.

As a step towards regulation, the British Nurses' Association was founded in 1888 by Ethel Fenwick. This was followed by the Society for the State Registration of Nurses in 1902 and two years later, the National Council of Nurses of Great Britain and Ireland. After years of campaigning by Fenwick and others, the Nurses' Registration Act was finally passed in 1919 and General Nursing Councils were formed in England, Wales, Scotland and Ireland in

1921. This means that the Central Register for Civilian Nurses does not begin until 1921, although it does include the names of women who qualified before this date. There was a distinction between a State Registered Nurse (SRN) and a State Enrolled Nurse (SEN). From 1940, SENs were formally recognised. They were not as highly qualified as the SRNs but had undergone two years' training. From 1983, the nursing register distinguished between those whose training reflected different specialisms, such as mental health, disability, midwifery and health visiting. Pupil nurses were those still undergoing training. District nurses, midwives and health visitors are all specific roles within the wider remit of nursing.

The Royal College of Nursing **www.rcn.org.uk** was founded in 1916 and developed into a trade union for the nursing profession. Its headquarters, at 20 Cavendish Square, London W1G 0RN, has a library and archive that includes books, journals and periodicals. A series of excellent guides to researching nurses can be downloaded from their website **www.rcn.org.uk/library/archives/family-history**. These give plenty of additional guidance for those who have nurses in the family. A number of nursing journals, from the early twentieth century, can also be searched and viewed from their website. The Royal College of Nursing's annual published records of state registered nurses 1922–1968, can be seen at TNA in class DT10. The Wellcome Library **http://archives.wellcome.ac.uk** holds records of the Queen's Nursing Institute (1887–1997) and these are available on Ancestry. They include the names of those who were submitted for appointment as Queen's Nurses (1891–1969) and registers of badge holders (1907–1945). There is interesting background information about the charity, which was founded using money from Queen Victoria's jubilee fund, on the Queen's Nursing Institute Heritage website **https://qniheritage.org.uk/history/the-queens-nursing-institute/**.

TNA also holds records of early nurses who were part of Elizabeth Fry's Nursing Institution, which was founded in the

1840s. This was the Protestant equivalent of the many Catholic institutions that provided care for the sick. Those run by the Catholic church were often convents and the nurses were also nuns. National Records of Scotland hold nursing registers for the period 1885–1930. If your ancestor worked as a matron or nurse in a Union Workhouse there may be relevant records with those of the institution concerned. Some General Nursing Council Registers are searchable on Ancestry: England and Wales 1922–1968; Scotland 1945–1948, 1950, 1955, 1957–1967; Ireland 1939, 1943, 1945–1948. For Northern Ireland, records for the 1940s and 1950s are also available.

The nurses who are easiest to track down are those who worked for the armed forces. A good starting point here are the research guides from TNA: *Doctors and Nurses*; *Military Nursing*; *Royal Air Force Nurses*; *British Army Nurses* and *Royal Navy Nurses*, which are available to be downloaded freely at **www.nationalarchives.gov.uk**. Records of military nurses from 1856–1994 are available on Findmypast **www.findmypast.co.uk**. These can be quite informative and may include information such as date of birth, father's occupation, where and when the nurse trained and the school she attended.

The Army Nursing Service was set up in 1881 and this was when the army first began to employ professionally trained nurses. In 1902, The Army Nursing Service became Queen Alexandra's Imperial Military Nursing Service (QAIMNS). It was renamed again in 1949 and became the Queen Alexandra's Royal Army Nursing Corps (QARANC). QAIMNS service records and those for the Queen Alexandra's Imperial Military Nursing Service (Reserve) QAIMNS(R) and the Territorial Force Nursing Service (TFNS) for 1902–1922 can be downloaded from TNA website. Records of medal holders are also available in this way. For records of those who served in QARANC during the Second World War, you have to contact the Ministry of Defence.

Until 1883, naval nurses were usually male, frequently former service personnel. Some women did nurse at the Royal Greenwich Hospital and this was often seen as a way in which seamen's widows could support themselves. There are some records of their applications 1817–1842 in class ADM 6 at TNA.

Although VAD (Voluntary Aid Detachment) nurses are associated in many people's minds with the First World War, they began in 1909. For plenty of background information and records of those who served during the First World War see the Red Cross website **https://vad.redcross.org.uk**.

It was not until 1943 that nursing training was fully regulated and the state registration of nurses became compulsory. Prior to this, it was not necessary to be trained in order to hire yourself out as a nurse and many nurses who appear to be living-in in late nineteenth- and early twentieth-century census households would not have been formally qualified. They might have been employed to look after a sick, elderly or disabled person, or they might be 'monthly nurses', attending to the newly delivered mother and baby. There were also wet nurses who would be employed to feed the babies of those who did not wish to breastfeed, or were unable to do so, and in circumstances where the mother had died.[2] Nursemaids were of course rather different and were regarded as domestic servants. Their role was to look after the nursery and its inhabitants.

Women used subterfuge and sometimes took drastic measures in order to be allowed to practice as doctors. Miranda Barry, assuming the name and persona of James Barry, qualified as a doctor in Edinburgh in 1812 and was able to practice, as it was not until her death, in 1865, that she was revealed to be a woman. Dr Elizabeth Blackwell became the first woman to register with the General Medical Council, in 1858, on the grounds of having studied at an American medical school. Elizabeth Garrett Anderson studied various aspects of medicine and as a result of her qualifications and the wording of their charter, the Worshipful Society of Apothecaries, the forerunner of the British Medical Association, was unable to refuse her a licence to practice on the grounds of her gender. They swiftly closed the loophole by refusing entrance to women.

The Medical Act of 1876 allowed for the licensing of men and women but there were still many barriers to women accessing a medical education. Even universities that allowed women to study might refuse to let them sit the qualifying examinations, or withhold the preferring of degrees. Sophia Jex Blake was one such; she received a certificate of proficiency, from Edinburgh University, in place of the medical degree that was bestowed on her male peers. Sophia continued her studies abroad, allowing her to finally be able to register with the General Medical Council. Together, Elizabeth Garrett Anderson and Sophia Jex Blake set up the London School of Medicine for Women, which was later to become the Royal Free Hospital School. This allowed women to train and graduate with the qualifications necessary to practice. The records are held at the London Archives.

By 1914, although training opportunities were limited, there were about 500 qualified women doctors in England and Wales. During the First World War, King's College Hospital, London was among a few who began to offer training to women. It was not until 1944 that the government forced the issue by denying funding to institutions that did not admit 'a reasonable proportion' of women. This was deemed to be 20 per cent and this figure was often regarded as a cap, rather than a minimum, making it much harder for women to gain a place as medical students, compared to their male counterparts.

There are copies of the Medical Register dating from 1859–1959 on Ancestry, but only every fourth year has been digitised. These give the names and addresses of doctors, their qualification and the date they registered. There are some additional paper copies at TNA. Medical Directories list both practising and retired doctors, although doctors did not have to be listed. The Wellcome Library holds original copies and TNA has copies for some years. Those for 1845–1942 can be searched on Ancestry. Registers of medical students, including students of dentistry, for 1882–1937 are also at the Wellcome Library and on Ancestry. Issues of *The British Medical Journal*, first published in 1840, are available online at **www.bmj.com/archive/**.

Prior to the mid-nineteenth century, caring for the sick was often the duty of the housewife, or the role of a lowly servant and as such, most of our female ancestors would have performed these tasks. Once it became possible for women to continue this role in a trained and qualified capacity, as nurses or doctors, many took this opportunity. While nursing was perceived, until very recently, as a 'woman's job', becoming a doctor, was regarded as an option for men. Women who wished to take this course faced obstacles and discrimination in order to do so.

Chapter 10

Feeding the Family

Food is obviously a necessity of life and although it might have been the role of the man of the family to hunt or farm the items on the menu, it was the woman's job to prepare it. In the past, our diet was limited by the availability of ingredients. Transporting food was difficult and therefore costly. Produce that was not grown or reared in the area would therefore be unobtainable, or very expensive. Until the agricultural improvements of the late eighteenth and early nineteenth centuries, growing seasons were much shorter than they are today. Problems with storage meant that foodstuffs might only be available during that very short growing season. Many foods that we now take for granted would have been unknown to our ancestors. Readers of more mature years will remember a time when each country had its own cuisine and the eating of 'foreign' food was virtually unknown. Many of us will have experienced childhoods without pizza, pasta or curry, a concept that twenty-first-century children greet with incredulity.

Before we look at what might have been on the menu, a word about quantities. Until the mid-twentieth century, when car ownership became more common and many began to swap manual work for more sedentary occupations, our ancestors led very physically active lives. It is likely that our great-grandparents and their forebears would have needed to consume double the number of calories of today's population, just to maintain their body weight. A major proportion of the family's time and budget would be devoted to the provision of food.

Filling up the family might be a problem both financially and practically. There would have been a smaller range of carbohydrates at the disposal of the housewife of the early 1600s, for example. If she was living in Britain, she would not be using pasta or rice, although a little wild rice might be available for puddings. Newly arrived potatoes were accessible only to the wealthy and the belief that they were a fruit meant that they were usually consumed when the skins were green. The resulting stomach ache did not encourage people to try this delicacy very often, so they were reserved for occasions when a rich host wanted to impress his dinner guests with his ability to be fashionable. Gradually, of course, potatoes became a key element on the menu and by the early nineteenth century, they were a cheap way of keeping the family fed. Porridge was eaten, particularly in Scotland, but the main staple was bread. A good housewife would bake a large 'gallon' loaf each day but Sunday and bread might constitute more than half of all the food the family consumed. If your ancestress was grinding her own flour, then this could take her up to an hour each day, her 'daily grind'. White 'manchet' bread required more refined flour, therefore was for the rich and as such was perceived to be more beneficial to health. The coarser brown bread was for the majority of the population. The further down the social scale you were, the darker your bread might be, with 'carter's' bread being the poorest sort.

What our ancestors might have eaten was also limited by the cooking methods available. For centuries, cooking was done over an open fire, either outside or in the centre of the home, with the smoke either escaping from a smoke-hole above the hearth or creating a layer of tar on the underside of the thatch. By the seventeenth century, brick- or stone-built chimneys were becoming more common in all but the very poorest of homes. Different fuels give different heats and therefore were more suitable for cooking certain things. Again, locally sourced fuel would be used. Although wood was the most usual, coal, peat, furze, dried animal dung and dried seaweed were also options. Coal was difficult to transport, but by the 1600s it was already being shipped from the coal fields around Newcastle to London.

By far the most common cooking method, until the nineteenth century, when stoves came into regular use, was the pot suspended over the open fire. In this early form of slow-cooking, available ingredients would be thrown into the pot to create 'pottage'. The pease pottage of the nursery rhyme was particularly common, as peas could be dried and thus stored. Roasting on a spit required a larger hearth, more fuel and a servant to turn the spit, so it was a method used by better-off families.

Iron stoves or ranges were first introduced in the mid-eighteenth century and most Victorian homes would have had a Bodley, or similar, stove. Initially, these were fired by wood or coal, but gradually they were replaced by gas stoves and in the twentieth century cleaner, electric cookers became popular. Utensils were treasured and valuable items. Pots and pans were usually iron and very heavy to lift. As families were large, cooking vessels were often sized to suit.

Preserving food was an essential skill for a housewife. Ice houses, which might be found in the grounds of the largest homes, were inefficient and refrigerators were not used in the domestic setting until the twentieth century, with many homes being without these items until the 1960s, or later. Separate freezers, as opposed to a small ice box within the fridge, came even later still. So what could our ancestresses do? Meat was often smoked or dried. Many chimneys had hooks for suspending joints of meat above the smoke of the fire. Fish too could be smoked, but sea fish would be rare if you lived away from the coast. Another method of storing fish was to salt it. Alternate layers of salt and fish would be laid in a barrel and sealed. A tap in the barrel would allow the brine to be drawn off. This was more common for oily fish such as herring and mackerel. White fish, particularly cod, were usually dried in the sun on racks. Some properties, notably farm houses, had butter wells where butter could be stored in brick or stone, well-like structures, where a spring or cold running water helped to keep produce cool.

Freshwater fish and eels were popular and larger households and farms might have their own fish ponds. The rearing of doves and rabbits for the table was also common. Game was eaten by the rich and by efficient poachers. Until the late nineteenth century, although chickens were eaten, they were primarily reared for their eggs, rather than their meat. Eggs were mostly used for baking, rather than being poached, boiled, scrambled or fried. Fruit, such as apples, could be sliced and dried. Other fruit would be bottled, or once sugar became more affordable in the nineteenth century, turned into jams. Pickling was another option for vegetables. A housewife would be expected to grow vegetables for the family and the produce of her dairy was another vital source of food. Dairying is covered in more detail in Chapter 12.

Nothing was wasted, quite a feat in times when left-overs could not be frozen. Cheaper cuts of meat would eke out the weekly budget and offal was frequently eaten. Another name for offal was 'umbles', hence the creation of umble, or humble, pie. Recalling the 1950s, ladies participating in a memories project wrote:

> Tripe was served up every three or four weeks, usually boiled in milk with chunks of onion but occasionally curried, which helped considerably! A relative had a tripe stall in Newcastle market and sold about fifteen different kinds of tripe, all of it disgusting (to me)! Sometimes Mum would get a sheep-head, which was split in two and she would use any traces of meat in stews; the brains were spooned out, mashed and served grilled on toast, rather like herring milts. Likewise, half a cow's head would provide meat for brawn and pressed tongue. Bones were slow boiled to give a nutritious stock for

soups and stews. Offal was served at least two or three times a week: sweetbreads, liver, and kidneys.

> I remember baked heart stuffed with onion but Mum's liver and onions with gravy was my favourite. I remember eating brains on toast once.[1]

Roast cow's udder was considered a delicacy in the seventeenth century and the amount of expensive spices that are used in this recipe illustrates that this was not a dish for the poor:

> Take a cow's udder and first boil it well, then stick it thick all over with cloves. Then when it is cold, spit it and lay it to the fire and apply it very well with basting of sweet butter and when it is sufficiently roasted and brown dredge it and draw it from the fire. Take vinegar and butter and put it on a chafing dish and coals and boil it with white bread crumbs, till it be thick. Then put to it a good store of sugar and cinnamon and putting it in a clean dish lay the cow's udder therein. Trim the sides of the dish with sugar and so serve it up.[2]

Tea, coffee and chocolate found their way into more popular use in Britain after the Restoration of the monarchy in 1660. Initially, they were viewed with suspicion and were drunk as part of a social ritual rather than to quench thirst. Herbal teas were drunk, but these were viewed as medicines rather than everyday beverages. Tea drinking gradually worked its way down the social scale and was more generally consumed in the nineteenth century, especially in the light of the Temperance movement. Some milk would have been drunk but it was primarily reserved for butter and cheese making. The drinking of water was not wise, as it often harboured disease. The science of germs was not understood until the 1860s and it was the Public Health Act of 1875 that took serious steps to ensure clean water supplies, especially in towns. The rich might drink wine or fortified spirits, while in apple- and pear-growing areas, cider and perry were available to all classes. Fruit wines might also be made by rural housewives.

Primarily, until the nineteenth century, our ancestors would have drunk ale or beer. The adding of hops or barley to the water and the subsequent boiling, made it safer to drink. Much of this beer had a very low alcoholic content and was known as 'small beer'. An eighteenth-century recipe for 'strong mead', an alternative beverage, demonstrates the complexity of its production:

> To four gallons of water, put eighteen pounds of honey; beat the whites of four eggs, stir them in with the honey till it all be melted; scum it well as long as it boils, and be sure it boils an hour and a half. If you like the taste, you may put a sprig of rosemary in the boiling. When it is cold, work it with a toast, spread with yeast; and when you put it in the vessel, hang therein one nutmeg, the weight of that in mace, and the same quantity in cloves, with four races of ginger, in a piece of muslin; the spice must be beaten; put in the peel of two lemons. When it has done working, stop it up, and let it stand six months, before you bottle it.[3]

In order to ensure that their families did not go hungry, our ancestresses' tasks ranged beyond basic cooking and food preparation to encompass brewing, dairying, gardening, beekeeping, preserving, pickling and butchering. No wonder that they needed to spend several hours each day feeding the family.

Chapter 11

Glove Making

Glove making was one of the various home industries that allowed many English women to combine paid employment with running a household. All types of gloves were produced, from workmen's gloves to those made from silk, lace, or velvet. Like most home industries, this was carried out on a piece-work basis. The cutting out was usually done in factories, often by men, and the cut pieces would be delivered, or collected from the cutters by the women, for sewing together. The women were paid by the number of gloves that they produced and gloves that required the greatest skill commanded the best rates. Silk gloves, and those with elaborate beaded decorations, were reserved for the most experienced workers, who would have been regarded as having reached the top of their trade.

It was not only the adult women who made gloves. Even after the advent of compulsory schooling, girls might work for up to four hours each evening after school, contributing to the family income by glove making. Although glove making was less suitable for young children than some other types of home work, because of the skill involved, the nimble fingers of 6- or 7-year-olds could help with the finishing by tying off and running in loose threads, even if they could not produce the small, even stitches that were required for the sewing.

Glove wearing, especially for women, was a sign of respectability and until the mid-twentieth century, all but the poorest women would expect to put on gloves when leaving the house. The fact that there was also a need for workmen's gloves and gloves for military uniforms meant that there was a steady demand. A charter of 1638 allowed the glovers to establish a guild that was separate from other leather sellers and, unusually, women were accepted as full members.

In 1784, it was proposed that a tax be placed on glove retailers, who would be obliged to pay for a licence or risk being fined. The levying of this duty was based on the assumption by the chancellor, William Pitt the Younger, that 9 million pairs might be sold each year. It was proposed that by imposing a tax of 1d a pair on the cheapest gloves, rising to 3d for more expensive gloves, £50,000 a year might be raised. It transpired that the actual revenue was closer to £6,000 a year and after ten years, the act was repealed.

There were various attempts to protect the glove trade from foreign competition. In 1826, the embargo on the importation of foreign gloves, which had been in place since the fifteenth century, was lifted, seriously damaging the trade and resulting in petitions for its reinstatement. The English glovers now had to compete with better quality gloves produced in France and Italy. Friendly Societies, such as The United Glovers Mutual Aid Society, based in Yeovil, and the Amalgamated Society of Glovers, worked to protect the glove workers. These two organisations amalgamated in 1920 to form the National Union of Glovers.

Gloving was the home industry of choice in several English counties including Somerset, Worcestershire, Devon (particularly North Devon), Wiltshire, Herefordshire, Oxfordshire and Leicestershire. Between 1790 and 1820, the thriving trade in Worcestershire, where about half of all English gloves were being made at that time, employed 30,000 people, many of whom would have been female home workers. As fashions changed, the demand for gloves fell. There are now so few glove makers that the making of hand-sewn, leather gloves is considered to be an endangered craft.

Some regions specialised in leather gloves, others in fabric. For example, Oxfordshire held the contract for leather army gloves and Leicestershire was particularly noted for woollen gloves. On

6 November 1847, the following item appeared in the *Illustrated London News*:

> The Town Council of Worcester has resolved to establish a school, in a convenient part of the city, for the instruction of young girls in the improved system of glove making, and four mistresses selected from the best workwomen to be found are to be appointed. By this means the work now sent to other towns at a distance (a good deal is sent in to Devonshire) will be done at home. It is computed that as much as £500 a week is sent out of Worcester to distant parts for payment of gloveresses alone.

This 'school' would almost certainly have restricted the education to gloving alone and would have been very unlikely to have included any lessons in literacy or numeracy.

Glove making could be highly skilled; it was difficult to produce even stitching and gloves of a consistent size. An invention of 1807, the gloving donkey, was first used in Somerset, one of the centres of the gloving industry. This contraption was worked by a foot pedal and the wooden stand contained rows of brass teeth that acted as a guide for the stitcher. It enabled the glover to work more quickly and with more uniform results. It fell into disuse with the invention of the sewing machine. Early treadle machines were available from the 1820s.

As the nineteenth century progressed, mechanisation became more common, which made home working less economically viable. Some women went to work in the glove factories instead; for others, this heralded the end of a valuable and often vital, source of income. Gradually, as sewing machines became more affordable, it once again became practical for women to sew gloves at home. The number of home-working glove makers began to decline in the twentieth century as glove wearing became less common and factories increasingly expected their workers to come to them. Nonetheless, advertisements for home-working glovers have been found as late as the 1970s.

The *Worcestershire Chronicle* of 23 January 1856 reported:

> A Gloveress sends us a letter complaining of the extremely low prices paid to female workers, which render it, she says, next to impossible to maintain themselves by honest labour. We fear that the evil, which we deplore but have no power to mitigate, proceeds from there being an excess of hands in proportion to the work to be performed.

In 1864, a report stated that it took between five and six hours to make a pair of gloves. At this time, the women were paid 3s 6d for a dozen pairs. This was probably about half what their agricultural labourer husbands might earn in a week. In the 1870s, 3¼d per pair is mentioned as a rate of pay but this would differ with the type of gloves produced. In 1885, it was estimated that a home-working gloveress could earn 6 shillings a week but she would have to work very long hours to achieve this. Their male counterparts, working in a factory environment producing gloves, were earning 15 shillings a week. In the early years of the twentieth century, 4–5 shillings a week was considered to be the average potential income from gloving at home, perhaps a third of the wage of a labouring man. In 1958, the National Union of Glove Workers, which operated from 1920–1971, campaigned for a pay rise of 4d an hour. They were granted a 1d for men and 3 farthings for women.

Like many home industries, glove making was not beneficial to the health of the women. Long hours of immobility affected the women's posture and working in cold, poorly lit conditions meant that they developed eye strain and chilblains.

In general, the middle classes approved of home working for the lower orders. It meant that married women were kept safely where they belonged – in the home – and they were not tempted to neglect their husbands and children. In some eyes, glove making was one of the more respectable home-working trades, especially if a worker rose to the level of sewing the more prestigious silk or velvet gloves. Not everyone approved, however. In common with those employed in other home-working trades, gloveresses also attracted a bad press and were associated with loose living. A local landowner vented his feelings in the *North Devon Journal* of 17 March 1859:

> I consider the glove trade the great curse of the town and neighbourhood of Great Torrington. I consider the gloving trade tends to demoralise the young girls engaged in it; totally unfits them for any honest occupation; they live at home with their parents, spend their earnings in dress, gin etc. They work at home all day and at night turn out on the town. If married, they are bad wives and improvident mothers and we cannot induce them, as formerly, to employ themselves in the healthy employment of agriculture. I believe bastardy is on the increase.

Despite the hard work and long hours involved, for many families, the money that their womenfolk earned by making gloves was an essential contribution towards the family's budget. This was an era when all women were expected to have basic sewing skills and those who were able to utilise these to produce the more elaborate gloves would be esteemed by their peers and valued by their families.

Lilian Norah Guard's Story

On 3 October 1882, Mary Guard née Kelly gave birth to her fifth child in a small cottage in St Giles in the Wood, a North Devon village near the town of Great Torrington. The baby was named Lilian Norah and was taken to the local church for baptism on 25

November. In all, Mary was to have seventeen children in a twenty-five-year period. Although eight died in infancy, it would have been difficult for Philip Guard, baby Lilian's father, a labourer, to support them all. Fortunately, the area around Great Torrington was well known for glove making. There were several glove-making factories in the town but the majority of the employees worked from home, Lilian's mother, Mary, among them.

Each week, the packman delivered the cut pieces and Mary Guard sewed them together, taking care to keep the stitches neat and even, as she would not be paid for sub-standard work. Some of the workers would walk to the factories to deliver their own work and collect the next week's raw materials and Mary may well have made the 6-mile return journey herself, perhaps accompanied by some of her growing number of children. It is likely that Lilian would have been enlisted to help boost her mother's output as soon as she was able, perhaps running in loose threads. Once the girls in the family were proficient enough, they too began sewing gloves.

Schooling was now compulsory, which reduced the girls' ability to earn and Lilian was duly enrolled in St Giles in the Wood School before she was 4 years old. Six months later, just after her fourth birthday, Lilian is noted as having left the school because the distance was too great to attend. No information was given about any future school. Perhaps it was at this point that the family moved into town. Interestingly, Philip Guard had been summonsed for not sending Lilian's older siblings to school in 1884. He was to be in trouble for a similar offence regarding his youngest children in 1905.

In 1891 the Guard family was living in Calf Street in Torrington. Fourteen-year-old Annie was making gloves, like her mother. By 1901, Lilian, or Lily as she was also known, at 18, was the oldest of the seven children who were still living at home. Although her mother and younger sister were now making shirt collars for a living, Lilian was a silk glove maker. Silk gloves were the preserve of the more skilled workers, as they were more difficult to sew. The following year, Lilian became pregnant and Beatrice May Guard was born in 1902.

In 1905, Lilian was once again expecting a child and shortly after the baby was born, she married the father, John Henry Turner, a silk weaver for the glove industry, whom she almost certainly met through work. The family set up home in Well Street, Torrington and Lilian and John went on to have eight more children.

The war years were sad ones for Lilian. Her 4-year-old son, John, had died at the end of 1913 and her brother, Archibald, died of fever on the eve of his twenty-first birthday in 1915, while serving with the 6th Devons in India. In 1918, Lilian lost another child when her daughter, Edith, aged 4, died. On the eve of the Armistice, Lilian's husband, John, died of heart failure; he was just 33 years old.

Lilian now needed to support herself and eight children under the age of 16. She continued to make gloves, while her eldest daughter went to live with Lilian's parents. As the family were living in just three rooms at 66 Well Street, in Torrington, this must have been a relief. By 1921, the two eldest boys were also in work. Lilian was not to have her mother's support for very long, as Mary Guard died in 1923. Given the status of the family, an unusually fulsome obituary appeared in the local paper, referring to the many mourners at the funeral, as well as commenting that Mary was a stalwart of the Salvation Army and that she had been ill for some time.

Lilian and some of her adult children then moved to 1 East Street in Torrington. In 1935, Lilian's own death was reported in the newspaper. She had gone to work as usual at Vaughan Tapscott's glove factory in White's Lane, just round the corner from her home but had collapsed at work. Attempts to administer what we now call CPR had failed to revive her. Vaughan Tapscott, initially Vaughan and Sons, opened in Torrington in the 1880s and at its height employed about 600 people, mostly women. It is likely that Lilian had worked for them for several decades, both as an outworker and in the factory. Her story illustrates just how important home working, such as gloving, was to the domestic economy, particularly for families that lacked a male breadwinner.

Interestingly, following up Lilian's children's lives may shed further light on her circumstances. After Lilian's death, some of her children continued to share the house at 1 East Street. Beatrice and her younger sister were working as gloveresses, but Henry and Eva, aged 33 and 29, were described in 1939 as incapacitated. Henry had been employed as an errand boy in 1921 and Eva had been at school but could this incapacity refer to some kind of disability, maybe something that was hereditary and might account for so many of Lilian's siblings dying in infancy?

Chapter 12

The Duties of the Dairy

Most of our ancestresses would have made butter and cheese for their own family until well into the nineteenth century, but for some, being a dairymaid was a full-time occupation. Whether production was for home consumption or a commercial venture, the techniques were broadly the same. The dairy farm was obviously producing on a much larger scale and this might be reflected in the equipment used and the place in which the processes were carried out.

Dairymaids were not the same as milkmaids. The latter had care of the cows and were responsible for milking, whereas it was the role of the dairymaid to make butter and cheese from the milk; if the establishment was small, the two roles might be combined.

On a farm, ideally, the dairy would be situated in the north-eastern corner of a range of buildings that might shield it from the sun from the south and west. Windows were often small and high, placed on the shady side of the building, allowing a flow of air. In some areas, it was common practice to build the dairy over a small stream, or to divert a stream through the centre of the building. This not only provided water but also helped to keep it cool. Even at a time when cottage floors were often hardened earth, the diary might be tiled, to keep it both clean and cool. Poorer housewives would not have the luxury of a purpose-built space for their dairying. Gervase Markham wrote of the need for cleanliness in the seventeenth-century dairy. The dairy was to be kept 'sweet and neat ... where not the least mote of filth may by any means appear, but all things either to the eye or nose so void of sourness or sluttishness that a prince's bedchamber must not exceed it'.[1] It was not just the dairy that was expected to be clean. Each day, after use, wooden dairying implements would need to be scrubbed, using salt and boiling water. They would then be placed in the sun to dry.

Although we normally associate cows with dairying, sheep and goats were occasionally kept for a similar purpose. Firstly, the cows were hand milked by the milkmaid. Making butter and cheese required a high standard of cleanliness, so, ideally, a dairymaid would not have close contact with the animals that provided her with her raw materials. On the other hand, the housewife with a smallholding would milk the family cow and then perform the duties of the dairymaid as well. It is difficult to generalise, but before selective breeding, according to Markham, a cow might be expected to give a gallon of milk at each milking. Working in a dairy was not always pleasant, as it needed to be cold and was frequently damp. Dairymaids, however, had a higher status than some other servants and a skilled dairymaid would be prized.

Butter and cheese were much easier to store and more valuable than unprocessed milk. Consequently, very little milk was drunk or used in its raw state. Although milk might be scalded, pasteurisation is a comparatively modern process and is associated with twentieth-century commercial dairying.

Today, one of the principal uses of butter is for spreading on bread, but historically, bread would be eaten dry, or dripping would have been used. Until the nineteenth century, butter was primarily used in baking. Initially, the milk was left in a pancheon, or setting dish. These shallow, earthenware dishes allowed the cream to rise to the top. A housewife who was butter making purely for the family and having perhaps only one cow, might need several days' milk to have enough to make it worth churning. As long as the weather was not too warm, the fact that some of the milk was not fresh added to the flavour. Once the milk had settled, the cream was drawn off the surface using skimmers. These were thin, saucer-shaped implements, commonly made of brass or wood, with holes to allow buttermilk to drain through.

Churning butter could take anything from twenty minutes to two hours. The very earliest method of churning was probably as simple as putting the milk in a tightly sewn animal skin and then shaking it. Three main styles of butter churn developed. The plunger variety has a long history and examples have been found from the Dark Ages. It consists of a tall wooden receptacle into which was 'plunged' the 'dasher'. This was a large stick with a flat circle of wood attached to the end and it would be pulled up and down rhythmically. There were small hand-held versions but most of these churns were larger and stood on the floor. Alternatively, from the eighteenth century onwards, barrel churns, resembling a barrel on a stand, which would be turned over, became more popular. Paddle churns are more recent still and these are box shaped, with a paddle inside that could be turned by means of a handle on the top. These might be made of earthenware, metal or glass, all of which were more hygienic than the wooden versions.

Whatever style of churn was used, a repetitive action was required and butter making was a wearying activity. Once churned, the butter would be squeezed to remove the excess 'buttermilk'. The butter might be wrapped in fine butter muslin for this part of the process. The buttermilk itself was not wasted; it could be added to the pig swill or drunk.

If butter making was for commercial purposes, it might be done all the year round, but most housewives confined their butter making to the spring, when the lush grass meant that the milk was at its creamiest. In 1719, Hannah Woolley had this to say on the subject:

> Provide your winter butter and cheese in the summer and the best time to put up your butter for the winter is the month of May, for then the air is most temperate and the butter

will take the salt better; however, it may be done any time between May and September.[2]

The butter was salted to aid preservation, patted into shape using butter pats and stored for the remainder of the year. Most farmers' wives marked their butter with a design, using a butter mould, so that it would be distinctive when sold at market.

Cheese was a staple of the diet; in Tudor and Stuart times it was known as 'white meat'. It was also a prized commodity; Samuel Pepys notoriously buried his Parmesan cheese to preserve it from the Great Fire of London. There were many kinds of cheese, some were suitable for storing for up to a year, others would need to be eaten fairly quickly. Markham refers to 'divers kinds' of cheese: 'new milk, or morrow milk cheese; nettle cheese; flatten milk cheese and eddish or aftermath cheese'.[3]

Cheese making was a year-round activity for both housewife and dairymaid. Rennet is required in order to make cheese. Normally this comes from the stomach of a young animal and some of the stock would be reared especially for this purpose. The animal needed to be slaughtered before it was weaned, perhaps at about two weeks old. There were also ways of creating plant-based rennet, for example by using the juice from stinging nettles.

The milk and rennet would be warmed over the fire, taking care not to let it get too hot, no easy task for those using an open fire. It was then left to stand and set into a curd that could be separated or cut to remove the whey. For a soft cheese, the curds were then hung in cheesecloth to drain. Hard cheese would keep for longer and for this, the curds would be put in a wooden cheese press and a weight would be placed on the top. The cheese needed to be turned daily and salt water would be wiped on the outside to create a rind.

William Hazlitt, in his 1886 book, *Old Cookery Books and Ancient Cuisine*, provides a cheese recipe:

The Queen's Cheese – Take six quarts of the best stroakings and let them stand till they are cold; then set two quarts of cream on the fire till 'tis ready to boil; then take it off and boil a quart of fair water and the yolks of two eggs and one spoonful of sugar and two spoonfuls of runnet [sic]; mingle all these together and stir it till 'tis blood warm. When the cheese is come, use it as other cheese; set it at night, and the third day ay the leaves of nettles under and over it. It must be turned and wiped and the nettles shifted every day and in three weeks it will be fit to eat. This cheese is made between Michaelmas and Alhallontide.[4]

Storing butter, milk and, to a lesser extent, cheese, in pre-refrigeration days was problematic. From the seventeenth century, wealthy households might have an ice house, usually a stone structure that was half submerged in the ground. Ice would be cut from the rivers or ponds during the winter but rarely lasted beyond late spring. Of course, foodstuffs could be kept cool in stone-shelved larders; marble or, less extravagantly, slate, worked particularly well. Another method of storage was to put butter and cheese in a container and lower it down the well. There were also butter wells constructed specifically for this purpose.

Dairying was just one more of the many tasks that housewives were expected to perform, but women often took great pride in the products of their dairy. A bonus was that, in many households, it was customary for any money made from selling excess butter or cheese to be retained by the housewife for her own purposes.

Chapter 13

Cleanliness is Next to Godliness

In the twenty-first century, the average UK house*hold*, not house*wife*, spends two to three hours a week cleaning.[1] Until well into the twentieth century, a lack of cleanliness about the home was regarded as a sign of moral weakness, or even a lack of religious fervour. Cleanliness really was next to Godliness and our female ancestresses exerted a great deal of effort trying to achieve a level of cleanliness that would win the approval of their neighbours. In the days before the availability of labour-saving devices, this was physically demanding and time-consuming in the extreme. Before electricity and internal water supplies arrived in our homes, cleaning was even more arduous. Open fires made rooms smoky and sooty; the coming of the industrial age, prior to Clean Air Acts, gave towns and therefore homes, an overlying layer of grime. Many housewives had husbands whose occupations were such that meant they would be bringing mud, coal dust, fish scales, sawdust or factory dirt into the home on a daily basis. It was a never-ending struggle to keep up standards. Wealthier households may have had servants to carry out cleaning tasks but the processes and products they used would have been similar.

Putting on a show was essential. Once homes had glass in their windows these needed to be clean, as, later in history, did any net curtains that might be on show. The windows might be polished with vinegar and screwed up brown paper or, later, newspaper. A clean façade was a sign of respectability; the front path would be swept and the doorstep cleaned. Sand was used for scrubbing the stone and 'firestones' or 'holystones' were also sold for this purpose.

Inside the home, floors needed to be cleaned. At least until the eighteenth century, it was not uncommon for livestock to share the living accommodation with the family when the weather was inclement. Hardened mud floors would be covered with straw, bracken or furze to absorb the cooking fat and other debris. Strongly scented herbs would be strewn on the floor to disguise any unpleasant smells and the straw would be held within the room by the threshold. Every few weeks, the straw would be swept out using a besom broom and replaced. Birch twigs and heather were favoured for making besoms, and lime, hazel or birch would form the handle. In dry weather, or when it was hot, water was used to 'lay the dust' on an earth floor.

More wealthy households might have wooden floorboards. Ox-gall, a mixture of bile from an ox and alcohol, was recommended for rubbing on greasy spots. This would then be left for a few hours before using a strong lye on the floor. Lye was made by dripping water through wood ash and it was very harsh on the hands of the user. Sand could be spread over the wooden floor before scrubbing. Wooden floors would also be polished or oiled. Once large rugs or carpets were used, different techniques were required. Rugs could be hung up outside and rigorously beaten. Tea leaves were recommended for scattering over carpets before being brushed off with a stiff broom. Carpet sweepers and early vacuum cleaners made an appearance in the nineteenth century, but it was several decades before they were widely available. *The English Woman's Domestic Magazine* of 1854 advised:

> After all the dust is taken out, tack your carpets down to the floor. Then mix half a pint of bullock's gall with two gallons of soft water; scrub it well with soap and this gall mixture; let it remain till dry – it will then look like new. Be careful your brush be not too hard.[2]

At a time when open fires were in continual use, chimneys had to be swept regularly to avoid the dangers of fire. If professional sweeps were not employed, a good way of cleaning a chimney was to use holly twigs attached to a rope, which would be taken to the roof and then hauled down the chimney. The stove and grate also needed to be cleaned and this was a particularly messy task, often referred to as 'black-leading', involving the use of liquid graphite. *Mrs Beeton's Book of Household Management*, first published in 1861, clearly expected that the cleaning of the stove would be the duty of the housemaid, rather than the housewife but advised that the daily procedure should be as follows:

> She should then lay a cloth (generally made of coarse wrapping) over the carpet in front of the stove, and on this should place her housemaid's box, containing black-lead brushes, leathers, emery-paper, cloth, black lead, and all the utensils necessary for cleaning a grate, with the cinder pail on the other side. She now sweeps up the ashes, and deposits them in her cinder pail, with a wire-sifter inside, and a closely fitting top. In this pail the cinders are sifted, and reserved for use in the kitchen or under the copper, only the ashes being thrown away. The cinders disposed of, she proceeds to black-lead the grate ... Brunswick black, is an excellent varnish for grates and may be prepared from 1lb of common asphaltum, ½ pint of linseed oil and 1 quart of oil of turpentine ... A day should never pass without the housemaid rubbing with a dry leather the polished parts of a grate, and also the fender and fire irons.[3]

Dusters could be fashioned from goose feathers and cleaning clothes made from old rags. Before polishes were made commercially available, polish would be home-made using beeswax; yet another task for the overworked housewife. Bedding might consist of nothing more than an old blanket, and bed-bugs became a problem. In 1695, the London firm of Messrs Tiffin and Son was founded and was dedicated to attempts to exterminate these pests.

Doing the dishes was another essential job. One way of solving the problem was to give dirty dishes to the dog, who would then lick them clean. Greasy dishes could also be wiped with a wisp of straw, or dipped in bran, which would be brushed off, taking the worst of the grease with it. The bran then made ideal pig food. Plates and cooking vessels of brass, pewter, or even china, were cleaned by rubbing them with an abrasive such as a fine sand or ground shells. The plant that some call horsetails (Equisetum) was also known as pewterwort and this was rubbed on pans to create a natural non-stick. Lye was used for washing silverware; later, proprietary polishes were sold to clean silver, brass or copper.

Those recalling their memories of housework in the period after the Second World War wrote:

> For many families, the chores had a daily or weekly routine that was strictly adhered to. As a young child, in 1946, I remember that housework was quite regimented. Monday – wash day, Tuesday – ironing, Wednesday – downstairs cleaning, Thursday – upstairs cleaning, Friday – baking, Saturday – cooking and odd jobs, e.g. mending, sewing etc., Sunday – day of rest.[4]

The annual ritual of spring cleaning also had its own rhythms:

> Spring cleaning was undertaken by most families. Some of the tasks that this involved would be unimaginable to modern housewives. Spring cleaning required that the rooms be emptied as far as possible and the carpets were taken outside and beaten. Sometimes they were sprinkled

with cold tea leaves 'to absorb the dust' before beating ... Spring cleaning was not to be relished and often put a strain on the household. One room would be tackled at a time, with all the furniture including wardrobes and other heavy items being moved and the whole room being thoroughly cleaned. Each room took about two days and was a time of trial for my mother and discomfort for the entire household. Winter curtains and blankets were trundled round to the launderette in the spring and then packed away with the ubiquitous mothballs to be resurrected in the autumn, and fresh chintzy ones hung.[5]

The advent of labour-saving devices often saved effort but not time as they required some degree of supervision:

The 1950s and 1960s saw many families gradually acquire items that made women's lives easier. The arrival of labour-saving devices meant that, by the early 1960s, the average number of hours per day spent on housework, including the preparation of meals, had fallen to eight. This was the era when the first fridge or vacuum cleaner often appeared in the home and devices to assist with the laundry were also within the scope of the budget of all but the poorest families. These appliances represented a significant financial outlay, even for richer families. In the early 1950s, a fridge cost more than ten times the average weekly wage. Unlike today, however, the expectation was that these devices would last, if not for a life time, then perhaps for twenty or thirty years.[6]

All in all, keeping the home cleaned to an acceptable standard took many hours and a great deal of physical energy. Only the most recent generations of our ancestors benefited from the increasing use of specialist equipment and commercially made cleaning products.

Chapter 14

Pillows, Bobbins and Pins: Lacemaking

Some claim that there is a reference to lacemaking in the Bible, as the King James' version of Isaiah 9 verse 9 reads, 'moreover they that work in fine flax and they that weave networks, shall be confounded'. It is, however, likely that lacemaking as we know it first became established in the fifteenth century, probably in Italy or Flanders and the techniques spread across Europe. The fact that it was decorative, rather than functional, made lace a luxury item. Gold and silver threads might be used for the most affluent customers, but threads were predominantly linen or silk, with cotton making an appearance later on. Lace might be used for collars, cuffs or braid in order to make a garment more luxurious. Later, lace was also used to augment home furnishings such as tablecloths, doilies and antimacassars; the latter were put over the back of arm chairs to keep men's hair oil, or macassar, from staining the upholstery.

The wearing of lace was a sign of status and it was preferred to embroidery for augmenting clothing. This was because the lace was an entity in itself, which was stitched on to the cloth and, more importantly, could later be detached and re-applied to a different garment. It might also be removed for washing. This meant that lace had a longevity that other forms of decoration did not and you may find mention of lace collars or cuffs being bequeathed in wills. By the reign of Elizabeth I, Britain was importing lace to the value of £10,000 a year.[1] Lace was also being made in England; Shakespeare refers to 'free maids that weave their threads with bone' in *Twelfth Night*.[2] The Elizabethan Poor Law required overseers of the poor to provide work for poor children and there is evidence that lacemaking was one such activity in Bedfordshire and Buckinghamshire.

A Dame School, Thomas George Webster (1800–1886) – N00427. (The National Gallery image in the public domain)

Pottery in the Making: The work of J. & G. Meakin Pottery, Hanley, Stoke-on-Trent. (Jack Bryson, Ministry of Information photographer, 1942, in the public domain)

Above left: Dorset button under construction. (© Janet Few)

Above right: Suffragette propaganda left on the lawn of an English country house where the prime minister, Herbert Asquith, was staying in 1909. (Clovelly Archive and History Group)

WSPU poster by Hilda Dallas, 1909. (Public domain)

Above: Mill worker. (Public domain)

Left: Old rags into new cloth: salvage in Britain, April 1942. (Richard Stone, Imperial War Museum, public domain)

Above left: Land Girls Audrey Prickett and Betty Long set a rat trap in a hay stack as part of their training on a Sussex farm during 1942. (Part of the Ministry of Information Second World War Official Collection)

Above right: Land Girls using a double saw to cut down a tree as part of their training at the Women's Land Army camp in Culford, Suffolk in 1943. (Part of the Ministry of Information Second World War Official Collection)

Right: Irons. (© Janet Few)

Below left: Drying clothes. (© Janet Few)

Below middle: Washing board. (© Janet Few)

Below right: Bucket and laundry bat. (© Janet Few)

Above left: The Confectioners c.1810, woodcut image. (Public domain)

Above right: The Victorian Shop, Morwellham Quay by Robin Drayton. (**www.geograph.org.uk/photo/3175985 CC BY-SA 2.0**, used under Creative Commons from Wikimedia Commons)

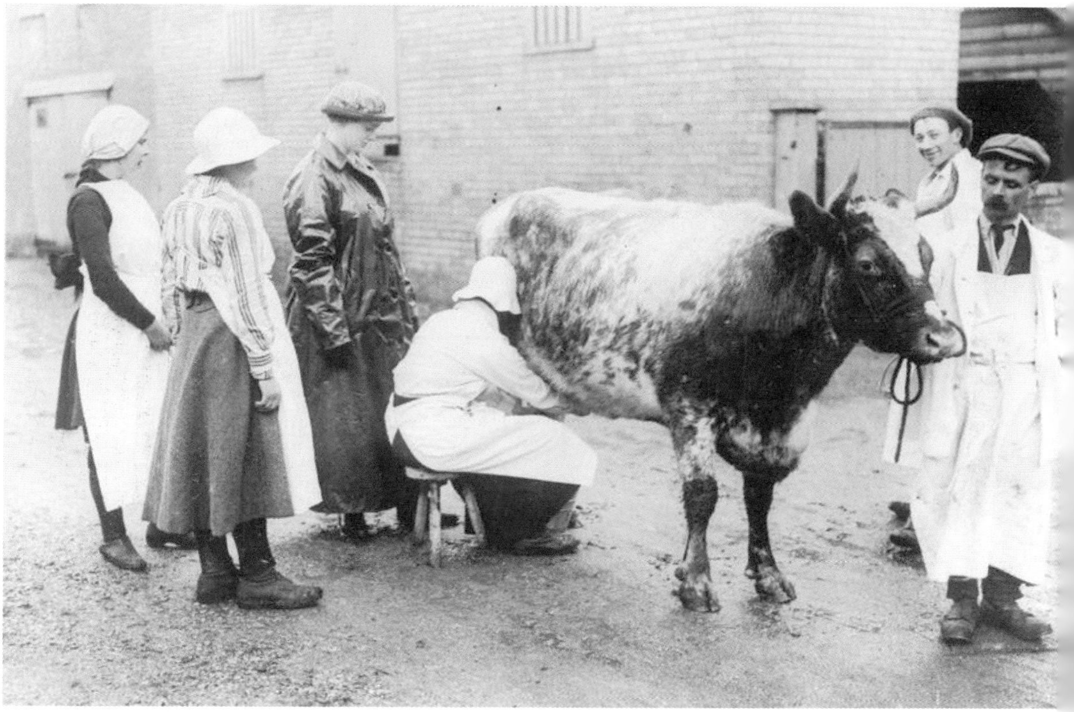

Women training to be milkmaids 1917. (This image was created and released by the Imperial War Museum on the IWM Non-Commercial Licence. Photographs taken, or artworks created, by a member of the forces during their active service duties are covered by Crown Copyright provisions. Faithful reproductions may be reused under that licence, which is considered expired fifty years after their creation)

Above left: From Samuel L. Goldenberg, *Lace: Its Origin and History*, Brentano's, 1904. (Public domain)

Above right: *The fireside university of modern invention, discovery, industry and art for home circle study and entertainment.* John McGovern from a catalogue of 1902. (Public domain)

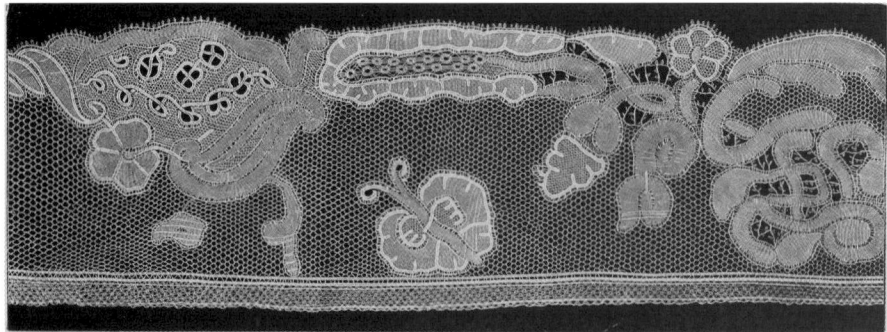

Above: From Mrs Bury Palliser, Margaret Jourdain and Alice Dryden, *The History of Lace*, Sampson, Low, Son and Marston, 1865. (Public domain)

Right: A woman giving birth on a birth chair. From Eucharius Rößlin, *Der Swangern frawen vnd hebamme(n) roszgarte(n)*. Hagenau: Gran, um 1515. (Public domain)

Sweeping the floor. (© Janet Few)

Pewterwort. (© Janet Few)

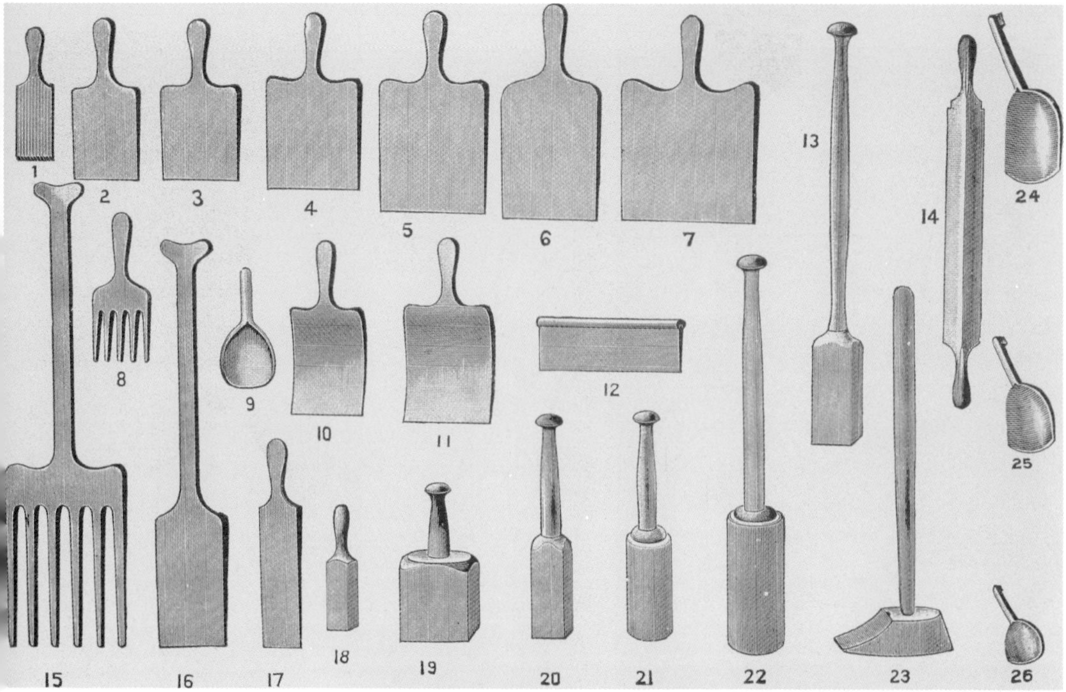

Above: Dairying apparatus, 1904. (Creamery Package Manufacturing Company, in the public domain, from Wikimedia Commons)

Right: Plunger or dasher churn. (© Janet Few)

Glove-making, c.1930s. (From the Collections of the Library of New South Wales SLNSW15423 used under Creative Commons)

A collection of gloves. (Documentation Centre and Textile Museum of Terrassa, used under Creative Commons)

Above left: Butter well. (© Janet Few)

Above right: Barrel churn by Musphot. (Used under Creative Commons CC BY-SA 3.0, from Wikimedia Commons)

Above: Kitchen at the old King Street Bakery, Frederick McCubbin, 1884. (Public domain)

Right: Hannah Glasse's Complete Art of Cookery. (Wellcome Collection. L0014987 used under Creative Commons Attribution 4.0, from Wikimedia Commons PD-1996)

Below: Twentieth-century cooking. (Public domain)

Left: Florence Nightingale. (Public domain)

Below: Naval nurses and the Red Cross train at Chatham. Wounded from Zeebrugge having their wounds dressed. (Wellcome Collection. L0009198 used under Creative Commons Attribution 4.0, from Wikimedia Commons PD-1996)

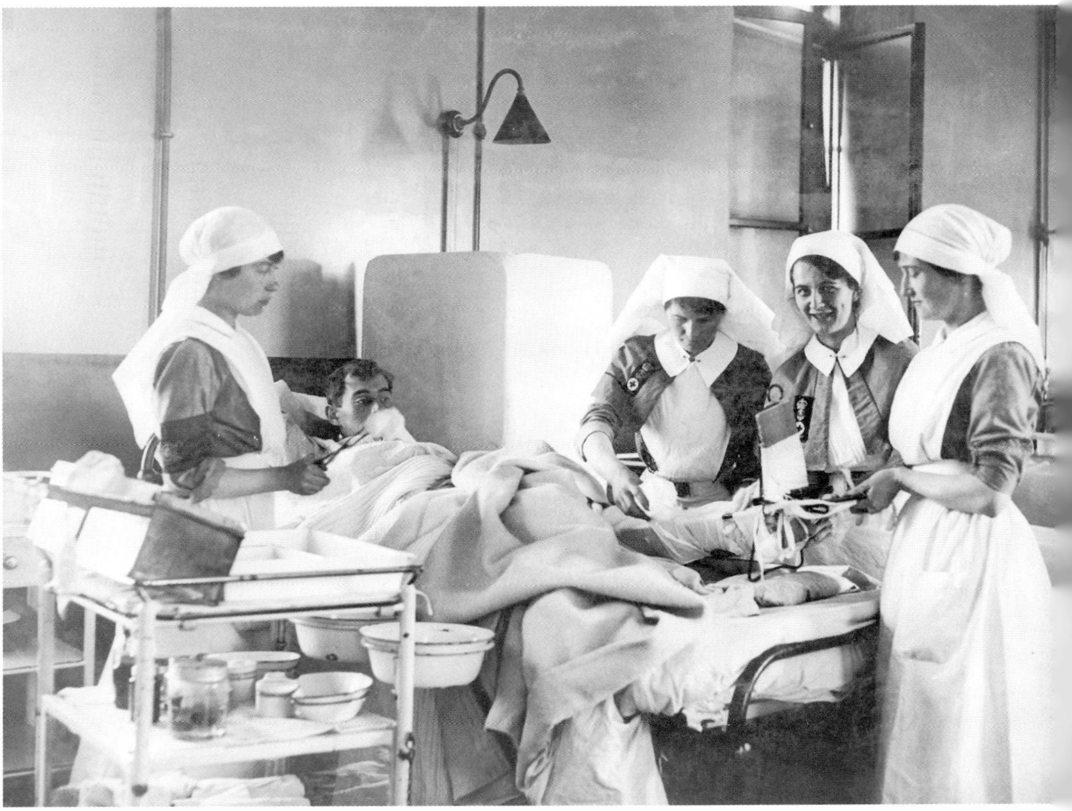

Above left: An alembic. (© Janet Few)

Above right: Dandelions. (© Janet Few)

 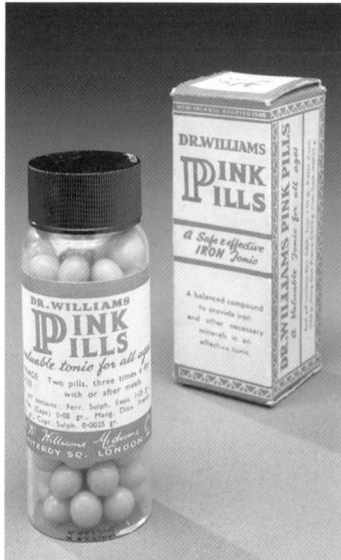

Above left: St John's Wort. (© Janet Few)

Above right: Dr Williams' Little Pink Pills, 1850–1920. (Wellcome Collection. L0058211 used under Creative Commons Attribution 4.0, from Wikimedia Commons PD-1996)

Left: A prostitute leading an old man into the bedroom and taking money from him; implying that her services will act like a tonic and preserve his state of health. T. Rowlandson, 1811. (Wellcome Collection. L0051171 used under Creative Commons Attribution 4.0, from Wikimedia Commons PD-1996)

Below: Herb garden. (© Janet Few)

Plait-school image by George Washington Brownlow. (Public domain)

Above left: *Shucking Oysters in Newhaven*, Hill & Adamson. (Public domain)

Above right: *Working in a Match Factory*, 1871 from *The Graphic*. (Public domain)

Left: *La Toilette*, Raimundo de Madrazo. (Public domain)

Below left: *Lady's Maid Ironing Lace, 1908*. (Library of Congress, in the public domain)

Below right: *The Scullery Maid*, Jean-Siméon Chardin, 1738. (Public domain)

Above left: Making clothes at home. (© Barbara Watts, used with permission)

Above right: Drop spindle. (© Janet Few)

The Munitions Girls by Stanhope Forbes, 1918. (Wellcome Collection. L0059548 used under Creative Commons Attribution 4.0, from Wikimedia Commons PD-1996)

There are two main lacemaking techniques, needle lace, with a single thread and bobbin, or pillow lace, which uses multiple threads. The earliest lace was created using merely a needle and thread. A pattern was drawn on to a heavy backing cloth, which was removed when the lace was finished, leaving the delicate openwork. Needle lace was largely superseded by bobbin lace, as it was possible to create similar effects and most forms of bobbin lace were much quicker than needle lace. Bobbin lace required the use of several threads attached to small turned wooden sticks, or bobbins. Early bobbins might also be made from carved bone. Intricately decorated bobbins could be given as a love gift. The threads were wound round pins that were stuck into a hard, straw-stuffed pillow, hence this form of lacemaking is also known as pillow lace. In the sixteenth century, pins were prohibitively expensive for some lace makers and fish bones or slivers of wood might be substituted; thus, occasionally, this type of lace is called bone lace. There are other, less common, forms of lace, such as knitted lace, which is famous in the Scottish Highlands. It was a feat to be able to create a lace shawl that could be drawn through a wedding ring in this way.

Different European towns are associated with slightly different designs of lace. In England, lacemaking was one of several home industries undertaken by women and girls on a piece-work basis. As with most of these trades, a skilled worker might earn a reasonable sum but may well be working a twelve-hour day in order to do so. Pillow lace workers were found predominantly in the home counties, such as Buckinghamshire, in the Midlands and in Devon, particularly South Devon. The towns of Nottingham and Honiton were highly regarded for the quality of their lace. The Honiton lacemaking tradition goes back to the seventeenth century. In 1676, it was claimed that there were 1,341 lace makers, including men, in Honiton itself and many more in the surrounding villages.[3] From the nineteenth century, the Isle of Wight, off England's south coast was also known for its lace, but this was largely machine lace.

In a similar way to some other home industries, lacemaking was often taught in lace 'schools'. These were not in any way educational establishments, but women and girls would gather together to make lace and to enable the children, some as young as 5, to learn from the more skilled workers. The intricate, close work often resulted in failing eyesight and sitting hunched over a pillow led to problems with posture. Government reports refer to the propensity to tuberculosis among young women in lacemaking areas and this was, in part, attributed to the humid atmosphere and lack of ventilation in the lace schools,[4] exacerbated by the charcoal burning 'dicky pots' that they used to keep warm. These were used in preference to an open fire, as the smuts and soot from a fire would discolour the lace.

It was not just the home workers who would know how to make lace. Some women would make lace for their own benefit and ladies' maids would be expected to craft invisible repairs to lace, even if they were unable to make it from scratch.

As with many repetitive tasks, the workers would chant rhymes, or sing songs, not only to alleviate the boredom but also to ensure that they kept up a steady rhythm. The nursery rhyme 'Jack be nimble, Jack be quick, Jack jump over the candlestick', is thought to be a lacemaking rhyme. Many of the lace makers' chants involve counting, such as: 'Nineteen long lines being over my door, The faster I work, I'll shorten my score, But if I do play, I'll stick to a stay, So Heigh Ho little fingers, I'll crank it away.'

The winds of change were twofold. Firstly, the Industrial Revolution brought mechanisation to lacemaking, along with many other aspects of clothing manufacture. Early machines date from the 1760s, and in 1809 a patent for a bobbin net machine was taken out by John Heathcote of Leicestershire. Lacemaking by hand was still highly prized, but for the most part, it became uneconomic. The lace industry was also subject to fluctuations in fashion and the trade plummeted in the early nineteenth century, when plainer gowns became the vogue. There was a brief revival when Queen Victoria used Honiton lace on her wedding gown, but the vibrant home industry of the eighteenth century was very much depleted by this point. Despite this, the Children's Employment Commission of 1860 recorded 150,000 British lace makers under the age of 15. The coming of compulsory education, in 1880, and various Factory Acts, limiting working hours, also played their part.

St Catherine's Day, 25 November, was dedicated to the lace makers, who traditionally would be given the day off and 'Cattern' cakes would be distributed. These were small fruit cakes flavoured with caraway and cinnamon. Allegedly, they were accompanied by a drink of 'Hot Pot', which was a mixture of rum, beer and raw egg. The custom of distributing cakes and the association with lace makers is attributed to Catherine of Aragon, who, when she was put aside as the wife of Henry VIII, is reputed to have destroyed all her lace and ordered the lace makers of Bedfordshire, where she was exiled, to produce replacements, thus giving them work.

Chapter 15

Midwifery and Childbirth

In the seventeenth century, approximately one in every forty births led to the death of the mother. As the average number of births for a married woman was six, pregnancy was a risk. There were four principal causes of maternal death. The first was puerperal pyrexia. This would set in three to ten days after childbirth, leading to pelvic abscesses. If the infection spread to the veins, as it habitually did, this would result in septicaemia, which was fatal. The most painful cases of childbed fever, as it was known, were those where the bacteria reached the fallopian tubes, causing peritonitis. Childbed fever was caused by a lack of cleanliness on the part of the doctor, the midwife, or those assisting at the birth, or was a result of failing to clean the instruments used. At a time when there was little recognition for the need for hygiene, the problem was exacerbated by the advent of lying-in hospitals, where birth attendants would go straight from one mother to another, without washing their hands.

In the 1790s, Alexander Gordon, a former naval surgeon, suggested that he and others helping during labour may be spreading infection. He recommended burning the bedclothes and fumigating the attendants. Ignaz Semmelweis published a work on childbed fever in 1858, in which he recommended the use of carbolic soap. These men faced ridicule; as a result, Gordon was forced to leave Aberdeen and return to the navy, while Semmelweis was committed to an asylum. In Semmelweis's case, his obdurate personality did nothing to help his ideas being accepted. The prevailing view of many mid-nineteenth-century doctors was summed up by Philadelphian obstetrician Charles Meigs: doctors 'are gentlemen ... a gentlemen's hands are clean'.[1] It was the work of Louis Pasteur, whose Germ Theory underpinned Joseph Lister's work on antiseptics in the 1860s, that began to make a difference.

Another cause of maternal death was haemorrhaging. Haemorrhaging that occurred before birth seriously weakened the mother and before the advent of safe blood transfusions in the twentieth century, excessive blood loss during childbirth was usually fatal. In the nineteenth century, Caesareans were often carried out in cases when maternal bleeding occurred before labour had begun. Unless the pregnancy was close to term, the baby was very unlikely to survive. Although Caesarean sections were rarely performed on a living mother until the early seventeenth century and then with very little chance of success, they were used for removing a child if the mother had died.

Death immediately following childbirth might also be caused by pre-eclampsia, or eclampsia, formerly called toxaemia, with high blood pressure leading to organ failure. Toxaemia could also kill before childbirth. This was, wrongly, thought to be associated with Bright's Disease, so this, or 'renal failure', might be recorded as the cause of death. The diagnostic signs are raised blood pressure and protein in the urine but it was not until the 1920s, and the instigation of regular blood pressure checks, that the condition was better understood.

The fourth cause of maternal death sprang from attempts to end a pregnancy, rather than from giving birth. In an era when there was no effective contraception, it was not just unmarried women who might be reluctant to go through a pregnancy. Legal terminations, carried out by medical professionals, were not available in Britain until 1938 and then only in very limited circumstances. This meant that women resorted to invasive procedures, often carried out in insanitary conditions, frequently leading to sepsis or blood loss that proved fatal.

Pain in childbirth was endorsed by the Bible, as it was seen as retribution for Eve's temptation of Adam. In 1856, Meigs wrote of the 'doubtful nature of any process that the physicians set up to contravene the operations of those natural and physiological forces that the Divinity has ordained us to enjoy or to suffer'.[2] Having been dissuaded against its use in previous labours, Queen Victoria famously used chloroform for the birth of her eighth child in 1853. Even after the queen helped to make the use of chloroform more acceptable, some doctors remained resistant and many mothers would not have had access to this luxury. Instead, they might have pulled on a towel tied to the bedposts at the head of the bed.

Although childbearing and childrearing did not warrant attention in Gervase Markham's *The English Housewife*, published in 1615, there was help for expectant and new mothers in the seventeenth century. In 1671, Jane Sharpe wrote *The Midwives' Book: or, the whole art of Midwifry Discovered*, later published as *The Compleat Midwives' Companion*. This was an expensive, illustrated book, aimed at the middle classes. It gave advice to those assisting at births and also covered such topics as conception, miscarriage and breastfeeding. Antenatal care was rudimentary and might consist of taking cinnamon, which was thought to bring forth lusty children.

The lying-in room was kept warm and dark and was not necessarily the sleeping chamber. Women were unlikely to give birth in bed. Instead, a squatting or kneeling position would be assumed and a birthing chair might be used. With the exception of the few male midwives, men were rarely present at a delivery. The mother was assisted by close women friends or relatives. These were known as her gossips, or god-sibs, the origin of godparents. The gossips were responsible for making a nourishing spiced ale, or caudle, for the mother.

Religion and superstition played a significant part in the day-to-day lives of our Stuart ancestors. The fear of childbirth meant that women relied heavily on prayers, or amulets, or both, at this time.

The churching of women, whereby new mothers attended a special church service shortly after birth, was practised in the seventeenth century. It was a ceremony that was seen to have Catholic overtones and was therefore frowned upon by the Puritans. Religious ceremonies following the birth of a child continue in many branches of the Christian church, although were much less common by the twentieth century.

In 1757, The Royal Maternity Charity for Delivering Poor Married Women in their own Habitations was founded by James Le Cour. Initially, its remit was to provide advice and maternity care for respectable poor women. In the late nineteenth century, cases of 'great necessity and destitution' might also receive financial and practical non-medical assistance from 'visiting ladies'. In 1905, the organisation set up a training school, preparing midwives for examinations. The charity's surviving records are held by the Royal College of Obstetricians and Gynaecologists.

Despite more awareness of the dangers of infection, childbirth was still a hazardous process in the 1890s. In Britain in this decade, one in every 200 pregnancies led to the death of the mother.[3] The infant mortality rate peaked at 15 per cent in 1893; this second highest ever recorded rate was attributed to increasing urbanisation.

The 1902 Midwives Act set out to regulate the training of midwives and, by 1905, all midwives had to register as 'bona fide' midwives, if they wanted to continue to call themselves midwives. By 1910, a bona fide midwife could only assist at a birth if she was accompanied by a certified midwife or a doctor. The 1902 Act also created the Central Midwives Board, to regulate practice and oversee training; its records are at TNA. Subsequent legislation between the wars continued to tighten the regulations, in order to ensure that those practising as midwives were suitably trained and qualified. They also laid out working conditions so, by 1936, there were improvements to pay and conditions, including days off and annual leave, midwives might expect one day off a month.

Some middle-aged women, who had had several children of their own, would gain a reputation for being an asset during deliveries and became the unofficial village midwife, although there were also licensed midwives. Professional medical help was usually only sought when the labour proved particularly difficult, by which time the mother was probably beyond all aid. The cost of this form of assistance was prohibitive for most families. Various herbal remedies might be used during labour, aquilegia and fennel both being recommended, but there was little that could be done if the delivery was not straightforward. Forceps were invented, by the Huguenot surgeon Peter Chamberlen, in the seventeenth century but they remained a closely guarded family secret for the next hundred years. His nephew, also Peter Chamberlen, attended the birth of the future Charles II.

The eighteenth century brought with it an increasing use of medical professionals during labour, particularly in wealthier households. This was the time of the accoucheur, the man-midwife. The introduction of forceps, regarded as a surgical instrument, had opened the door to male midwives as only members of the Guild of Barber Surgeons were permitted to use medical instruments. Nonetheless, births where the mother was assisted purely by untrained, female friends, neighbours and family members were still the norm.

Wet nurses might be hired by middle-class families and in cases where the mother had died, or was unable to feed the baby herself. Hannah Woolley's guidance for wet nurses gives specific instructions that they should abstain from spicy foods, take moderate exercise and refrain from copulation because 'it retracts, diminishes, and makes her milk to be an unsavoury taste, rendering it hot, rank or goatish, which is very prejudicial to the infant'.[4]

Advice, given in various manuals, provides an idea of the childbirth practices at the end of the Victorian period, although it may be that some of these suggestions would not have been adhered to if there was no professional midwife present. *Coming Motherhood*, written by Louis Spaeth and published in America, recommended how the mother should dress during labour:

> Probably the best way to dress a woman for the lying-in-bed is in short undershirt or under vest, shirt waist[5] and a skirt or petticoat, warm stockings and bed-room slippers. The supreme advantage of this method of dressing lies in the fact of the easy removal of the soiled garments. When labour is over, the skirt or petticoat is removed over the feet, the shirt waist taken off, and a clean night gown put on.[6]

Other preparations that were advised were a soap and water enema and plaiting the hair. Pads of newspaper were put on the bed to save the mattress. Although some of his comments seem to be directed to the mothers themselves, it seems Spaeth's book was aimed at healthcare professionals, rather than individual labouring women. It may be that the mother would have been encouraged to lie on her side for the final stages of labour. Following childbirth, the placenta would be burnt on the fire and the mother would be encouraged to rest in bed for at least two weeks.

Henry Davidson Fry, writing in 1907, dictated:

> The nurse should give particular attention to cleansing and preparing the skin of the abdomen, thighs, and external genital parts. First scrub with warm sterile water and soap, then rub dry, and afterward bathe the parts in a bichloride solution 1-1000, or solution of Lysol,[7] 1 per cent. It is particularly difficult to render the external parts surgically clean. The hair around the genitalia should be cut short with scissors or shaved, scrubbed with hot sterile water, and bathed with bichloride solution.[8]

Some of Louis Spaeth's advice sounds surprisingly modern, although couched in the language of an earlier era:

> Don't worry. Don't hurry. Simplify. Spend less nervous energy each day than you make. Work well while you work but don't be a slave. Avoid passion and excitement. Associate with healthy people; health is contagious as well as disease. Be cheerful; laugh. Eat plain food only. Drink nothing but plain water. Take a friction bath with a coarse towel, or a tepid sponge bath every morning. Exercise several times daily. Spend at least an hour daily in some out-of-door pastime, such as walking, riding, boating, or in other sports or games.[9]

How much of this advice weary working-class mothers, who probably had older children to attend to, would have been able to follow is debateable.

Mary Rake's Story

In February 1895, the press reported that Mrs Mildred Mary Rake, a 36-year-old midwife, of Malden Crescent, Kentish Town, had appeared at Marylebone Police Court, charged with the manslaughter of Mrs Hilda Grey, a labourer's wife. The issue was highlighted when an inquest following Mrs Grey's death found that the midwife, initially called Mary Rake in the newspaper reports and called Mary here for clarity, had been in attendance. Having assisted Mrs Grey at her confinement for her third child, Mary had asked another midwife, Mrs Henderson, to look after her patients, saying that she, Mary, had to go away for a fortnight. Dr Long confirmed that the cause of Mrs Grey's death was puerperal fever and peritonitis. The doctor also attested that Mary Rake had other patients who had puerperal fever and one had died that morning. He had advised Mary not to attend any more patients until she was clear of infection and to hand her patients over, which it seems Mary had done. Dr Sykes, Paddington's Medical Officer of Health, identified three recent deaths in childbirth in the area, in all of which Mary had been acting as midwife. Two more deaths followed. He wrote to Mary requesting that she did not attend any more births, for fear of the infection spreading. One of these other deaths was that of 25-year-old Helen, or Ellen, Beeken.

On 9 April, Mary was before the judge at the Old Bailey. Mary's 13-year-old daughter was called as a witness and said that her mother frequently disinfected herself and her clothes; other witnesses attested to Mary's good character. Her defence lawyer suggested that this was a case of an error of judgement, not criminal negligence. The jury debated for an hour but found themselves unable to reach a verdict and Mary was released on bail. On 24 April 1895, Mildred Mary Rake was charged on two indictments with the manslaughter of Ellen Beeken and Hilda Grey; no evidence was offered and she was found not guilty.

This was not Mary's first court appearance. The previous summer, she had been a witness in the trial of William Douglas Aitchison, who was accused of murdering his wife, Helen. On this occasion, Mildred Mary Rake's address was given as Malden Crescent. Mary had attended Helen Aitchison's confinement in her capacity as a midwife for the Royal Maternity Charity. The birth had gone well but the mother did not receive the food recommended by Mary. When she suggested that Mr Aitchison summon the doctor to see his wife, the husband responded with, 'I will cut her head off and trample on it.' Mrs Aitchison begged Mary to humour Mr Aitchison.

Nine days later, the nurse, who was attending the new mother, expressed concerns about Mrs Aitchison's health and the doctor was summoned. Helen Aitchison was found to have bruises and seemed in fear of her husband, who had spent time in the local asylum, where he had been violent to the attendants. Helen died shortly afterwards and the official cause of death was stated to be 'imperfect nurture and nervous prostration', as it could not be proven that her injuries contributed to her death.

Tracing Mary (or Mildred Mary) through the records was not a straightforward task. Census records over the decades record Mary's birthplace in three different countries and she gave birth in yet another country. Her forename and date of birth are also inconsistent and to add to the confusion, another Mildred Rake was also a midwife and both women were married to an Edward. Once it was established that these were two different individuals, a picture began to emerge.

Mary, initially referred to as Mary Ann, was the daughter of Charles Wade and was almost certainly born in South Africa, probably because her father was in the army. It is likely that she was only about 15 or 16 when she married Edward Rake, in Nusseerabad, India. Their son, Edward Archibald, was born in Nusseerabad in December 1872 but Edward and Mary Ann, or Marian, did not marry until the following March. Perhaps there was no one available to perform the ceremony any sooner. Their daughter, Ethel Margaret, was born in 1875 but only lived for a few days. By the time their son Charles Patrick was born in 1879, Edward was stationed in Dagshai.

In the 1881 census, Edward, 'Mary Ann' and their sons were in army barracks in Aldershot and Mary was claiming to have been born in Athlone, Ireland. Edward was a colour sergeant with the 2nd Battalion of East Lancashire Regiment. While they were in Aldershot, their daughter Violet was born. The youngest child, Talbot Eustace, was born in 1888 in Mile End, London and by 1891, the family was living at 10 Malden Crescent in St Pancras. Edward had retired from the army and was a club servant. 'Marian' was listed as a midwife and she appears as such in trade directories from 1895 until 1902.

Edward Rake died in 1900 and Mary and Violet moved into two rooms at 27 Malden Crescent, while Mary continued her work as a midwife. It seems that her accusation had not halted her career. All did not go well, however, as 20-year-old Violet became pregnant by a 40-year-old soldier, Harold Edward Sherwin Holt, and gave birth in 1902, perhaps attended by her mother. Directories show that the family then moved to 118 Prince of Wales Road in Kentish Town, London. Violet married Robert Henry Lairde Irvine two years later.

Under the terms of the 1902 Midwives Act, all those practising as midwives had to enrol with the Central Midwives Board in order to continue practising. As an untrained 'bona fide' midwife, in December 1904, Mary Marion Rake of 118 Prince of Wales Road was duly enrolled on the Midwives Roll, with the note 'in practice July 1901'. By the time of the 1907 roll, she was living at 26 Maitland Park Villas, Camden. Mary continued to move round London and the next listed address was 6 Brondesbury Villas, in Kilburn, where she was recorded in 1910.

In a complete change of lifestyle, Mary apparently retired and went to live with her daughter and granddaughter on the south coast, where, in 1911, Violet was running a boarding house in Broad Street, Brighton. This may well be because, from 1910, Mary would no longer be able to practice without the supervision of a trained midwife. Although Violet was listed as married, there was no sign of her husband who had petitioned for divorce in 1911 on the grounds of Violet's adultery. She had apparently, from 1909, habitually cohabited with one Charles Palmer, who had subsequently died. Violet's ex-husband died two years later. Divorce was very unusual at this time, particularly for those of Violet's social standing.

The time in Brighton was short lived, probably because the First World War would have impacted on the seaside boarding house business. It does not seem that either Mary or Violet used their nursing skills as part of the Voluntary Aid Detachment, although, by 1921, Violet was back in London, living with her unmarried brother, Charles, and working as a nurse. Interestingly, there is also an Emily Palmer from Brighton, who was one of several boarders in the household and possibly a relative of Charles Palmer. Violet was recorded in the 1939 register as being divorced. She was also listed as a 'former CMB (Central Midwives Board) Nurse', so it seems that she followed in her mother's footsteps.

Mary died on 7 October 1918, of a strangulated hernia, at St George's Hospital in London, with her daughter in attendance. She had been living at 6 Ebbsfleet Road, the home of her son Charles. Her working life was honoured to the last, with her occupation being listed as 'midwife (retired)'.

Chapter 16

Shopworkers

While the vast majority of working women were employed as domestic servants, by the later 1800s, a significant number served in shops. The nineteenth century saw the move away from the weekly market as the main place to purchase goods and the permanent shop become the predominant retail outlet, even in rural areas. There were two distinct types of shop work, which offered very different working environments. Firstly, there were those women who worked in small, often family-run, village shops. Widows or unmarried women, for whom a source of income would be essential, might support themselves by running the village store, a milliner's, or haberdasher's. Others acted as, frequently unpaid, assistants to their grocer or ironmonger husbands.

The role of the village postmistress was another job opportunity for women. This was usually on a sub-postmistress basis, so the women were not employed by the Post Office but ran a shop that provided post office services. This pre-dated the earliest employment of women by the Post Office, which began in 1870, with many women working to implement the telegraph system. Although Post Office employees had to be unmarried, the marriage bar did not apply to sub-postmistresses. Village or corner shop hours might be long but usually these women were living on the premises and could combine minding the shop with childcare and other domestic duties. They would be very much part of the local community, with the chance to pass the time of day with their customers.

With the rise of the newly wealthy middle classes in the nineteenth century, the shopping experience in towns was set to change. Until the Victorian period, shopworkers were traditionally male. The draper, greengrocer or butcher, would take on one or two assistants and perhaps train up a male apprentice. This model was no longer sufficient. The increasingly sophisticated, urban-dwelling female shoppers demanded the convenience and opulence of the large department store. At first, as these stores were opening, the tradition for male workers remained. Even exclusively female products, such as ribbons and stockings, might be served by a man. It was felt that women were insufficiently physically robust for the work and it was a widely held view that women's brains could not cope with the mental arithmetic required.

The Langham Place Group was formed in 1859 to campaign for employment rights for women, particularly in the professions. It also took up the cause of equal opportunities in the retail sector. It advocated the creation of special schools, where girls could learn the skills necessary to equip themselves for shop work. Of paramount importance was politeness to the customers, but other training was to include how to fold garments neatly and securing tidy parcels that would hold purchases safely. As it became the norm to employ women, which was, after all, the cheaper alternative, thousands of young girls, often from rural backgrounds, flocked to work in shops in the major towns and a new type of shop girl emerged. Shop work was considered to be preferable to domestic service, akin to a white-collar, clerical job for a man. An article in the *Manchester Courier*, in 1877, commented on the career choice of becoming a 'counter-woman':

> There are many plausible reasons for this selection, which carry great weight, especially with parents of young girls whose one aim in life is to appear 'genteel.' It is not a menial occupation. One may appear in it fashionably attired, and with hair arranged after the latest mode. Earrings and a brooch are not objected to, and – more precious than all – it is the

invariable rule at such places never to address employees by their Christian names. In domestic service this is oft-times the bitterest part of the portion a high-spirited young housemaid is made to swallow.[1]

Yet it was still not precisely respectable, with there being a strict social divide between customer and assistant. The newspaper article does go on to outline the many drawbacks of the occupation.

William Whitely from Leeds played an important role in the history of shopping and his regime was typical of many of the large department stores that had sprung up. By 1875, Whitely already owned several shops and 15 years later he had 6,000 employees, the majority of whom were young females. The women worked sixteen-hour days, from 7 a.m. until 11 p.m., six days a week. These long hours were punctuated with perhaps no more than a half-hour break for dinner and even less for tea. As the busiest times were late morning and early afternoon, the meal breaks had to be staggered and some girls found themselves eating at unusual times. This regime took its toll on the health of the girls, especially as they were expected to stand at all times.

Most large stores required their shop girls to live-in and the women were expected to pay for the food that was provided, which was often of an inferior quality. Some shops expected their workers to wear a uniform, which the girls might have to provide for themselves. There was also a stringent system of fines imposed for misdemeanours and these too had to come from their minimal wages. The Truck Act of 1831 forbade the practice of 'rewarding' employees in kind in lieu of wages, for example by giving them credit that could only be spent in factory-owned shops. Despite later amendments to the act, this legislation did not extend to shopworkers.

As late as 1906, it was estimated that more than 400,000 British shopworkers were still bound by some form of unacceptable payment in kind, such as the provision of substandard accommodation, where several girls might have to share a dormitory and probably also a bed. The living conditions were also injurious to health, with inadequate water and sanitation. Complaints to the Shop Assistants' Union, founded in 1891, wrote of the lack of heating and damp rooms, and diseases such as tuberculosis were rife. If the girls did get an evening or afternoon off, some shop owners would only allow them to leave the staff accommodation for a specific purpose and might require a written request from a suitable person, such as a parent or guardian, before permission for leave was granted. In 1877, London's *Bon Marché* store was built to include fifty bedrooms for staff. This marked a distinct improvement on the accommodation provided by other stores.

There were moves to improve conditions for those working in shops. The Early Closing Association was formed in the UK in the 1840s and the concept spread to America and Australia. It was not until 1912, however, that regular half-day closing was introduced in Britain. In 1891, it was estimated that there were more than 700,000 shopworkers in Britain. Meetings were held in Birmingham and Manchester, which resulted in the formation of a trade union for shopworkers. By 1947, this was known as the Union of Shop, Distributive and Allied Workers (USDAW).

The Shop Hours Acts of 1892 and 1895 stated that no one under the age of 18 could be employed in a shop for more than seventy-four hours a week, including meal breaks. This still permitted excessively long working hours and there were no limitations for older women. Amendments to the acts in 1898 did extend the limits to all women and reduced the hours for young women to sixty per week, with two hours a day for meals.

In 1899, the Seats for Shop Assistants Act introduced the idea that it might be desirable for shop assistants to sit when not actually attending to a customer. It was stated that one seat should be provided behind the counter for every three women employed. Fines for non-compliance were legislated for but this act was rarely enforced. In the first year, nearly 8,000 infringements were reported by London inspectors but only 630 cautions were issued and just a tenth of these led to legal proceedings. In 1912, the Shop Act required all shops to have a half-day closing; prior to this it had only been enforceable if two-thirds of the retailers in a town agreed. Even then, each council could exempt particular types of shop from the necessity to close early. The same act restricted late opening and from this time, most shops closed at 7 p.m., with late opening, until 8 p.m., on one day a week.

Apart from census entries, it is often difficult to trace the working lives of shopworkers. Larger stores may have kept employment records, or had in-house magazines. Women who joined the Shop Assistants' Union might appear in their records, but for the most part, these seem to have been kept on a regional basis and access is patchy. Sub-postmistress would not normally appear in Post Office records, as they were not employees. Women who ran the local post office often remained in the role for many years and their retirement, along with that of other long-standing shopworkers, might be reported in the newspapers.

Despite the aura of respectability that came with employment in a shop, the work was physically demanding, particularly in the large stores. A few women managed to gain promotion and act in a supervisory role, as floor walkers, others might become buyers. For most though, it was a source of income that they viewed as more desirable to domestic service but it was none the less arduous. In addition, the necessity to be polite to demanding, and sometimes irrational, customers at all times, meant that it could be as demeaning as being in service.

Chapter 17

Women in Wartime: The Land Army

The First World War

During wartime, the ability to import foodstuffs into Britain was compromised. The problem of ensuring that there was sufficient food was compounded because so many agricultural workers were away in the forces. Although agricultural work was considered to be a reserved occupation, there was still a significant labour shortage, making the recruiting of a female workforce a necessity.

The Women's Land Army (WLA) is more usually associated with the Second World War but women were also recruited for farm work during the First World War. It is estimated that, by 1915, ¼ million British women were working on farms. These were almost certainly women from farming families who were doing the work of their menfolk. The Women's National Land Service Corps was a voluntary organisation, formed in February 1916 but this failed to encourage enough volunteers. The Board of Agriculture created the WLA in January 1917, under the directorship of Dame Meriel Talbot. This organisation recruited 23,000 women; its stated aim was to increase the number of women working on the land and to ensure their efficiency and employment.

The recruitment of women was regarded with suspicion by many. It took visits from government officials before some farmers could be persuaded to take on a female labourer. Another issue was the regulation uniform, which, with practicality in mind, included trousers. This was viewed as unacceptable by many on moral grounds; women should not be wearing men's clothing. The Land Army Agricultural Section Handbook addressed this issue:

> You are doing a man's work and so you're dressed rather like a man, but remember just because you wear a smock and breeches you should take care to behave like a British girl who expects chivalry and respect from everyone she meets.

There was a positive campaign to recruit women from the middle classes, in the belief that this would have a propaganda value. It was anticipated that these women would become Gang Leaders, in charge of three or four other girls. Following an interview and medical, volunteers were expected to sign on for six months. After four to six weeks' training the women could earn 18 shillings a week. If they passed an efficiency test, they received an additional 2 shillings. By September 1917, 247 training centres and 140 'practice farms' were in operation. Training focused on one of three aspects: agriculture, timber cutting or forage. Those specialising in agriculture were taught animal husbandry, how to work with farm horses and the use of farm implements. Some were even taught to drive tractors, which were just coming into use on some farms. Forestry skills included felling trees and operating saw mills in order to produce duck boards for trenches, pit props and telegraph poles. Those intended for forage duties were taught to work steam-driven baling machines and to cut chaff. Forage workers were most likely to be assigned to a mobile gang that would travel from farm to farm.

The WLA was disbanded when the hostilities ceased. Correspondence and other papers relating to the Land Army in the First World War can be found in class MAF 42 at TNA.

The Second World War

With the prospect of war looming, the British WLA was reformed in June 1939 under the auspices of the Ministry of Agriculture and Fisheries. Their numbers were swelled when the conscription of women began in December 1941. As in the First World War, the women were interviewed and given a rudimentary medical to assess their fitness. Women could volunteer from the age of 17 and were likely to be unmarried and therefore free to be sent where needed. They were allowed to nominate a preferred location and were asked to specify two areas.

A propaganda campaign attracted many women into the WLA, often these were town-dwelling women, with little knowledge of the countryside. It is estimated that about a third of the land girls were from large industrial areas. Some took to their duties, others found it challenging. The work was strenuous and the days were long – forty-eight hours a week in winter and fifty in summer. For some though, the fresh air and comparatively good diet was welcome.

Tasks undertaken by the women included planting and harvesting crops, fruit picking, animal husbandry and dairying. Others worked in market gardening or formed vermin patrols to control pests such as foxes, rabbits, rats and moles.

Many of the land girls lived as part of the family with their employers, but there was not always sufficient space for them to do this. The government therefore set up a number of hostels to accommodate the workforce. For some, the living quarters were sub-standard. The pay was minimal. At the beginning of the Second World War, the average pay was 14 shillings a week, with the free board and lodging being valued at an additional 14 shillings. As was common in many working environments, men performing identical tasks would be paid 10 shillings a week more.

The uniform consisted of heavy brown leather shoes and a wide-brimmed hat, which was meant to be worn squarely on the head. Each woman was issued with three pairs of long, mustard-coloured knitted socks, three shirts in a heavy material, knee-length breeches and two green woollen jumpers.

A parallel service, the Women's Timber Corps, was set up, recruiting 'Lumber Jills' to forestry work. This was particularly vital as the German occupation of Norway had dried up one of the country's major sources of timber. Some 6,000 women are believed to have served in this way, enabling Britain to produce 60 per cent of its own timber by 1942. This freed up the shipping space that might otherwise have been taken up for the importation of wood.

Unfortunately, the service records for those who served in the British Women's Land Army in the Second World War have not survived. The Imperial War Museum has index cards relating to those who served between 1939 and 1950 and these are available on Findmypast. TNA holds microfiche copies of these alphabetical index cards from 1939 to 1948, in class MAF 421. They contain only very basic information: name, address, date of birth and Women's Land Army number. A few give details of transfers and demobilisation date. Details of the Women's Land Army and Timber Corps in Scotland can be found on Scotland's People **www.scotlandspeople.gov.uk/guides/record-guides/Scottish-Womens-Land-Army-records**.

In all, over 80,000 women served in the WLA during the Second World War. They undertook duties that were every bit as significant as those performed by their male counterparts and it is important that we honour and respect their contribution.

Chapter 18

Monday's Wash Day: Laundry Through the Ages

Taking in laundry was an option for women who needed to earn extra money from home and the techniques would be similar to those described here but on a larger scale. As more commercial laundries began to be established in the nineteenth century, these provided other employment opportunities for women. This chapter though concentrates on the tasks of the housewife who needed to undertake the family's weekly wash.

Why *is* Monday wash day? Traditionally, clean clothing was donned for the weekly visit to church on Sunday, when the family was on display and needed to look their best. In the days before mechanical driers, washing on a Monday gave the housewife the longest possible time to get the clothes dry, before they were required the following week. It is only in recent decades that the custom of washing on a Monday has become a thing of the past. Let us journey back through the generations to investigate what this arduous task would have involved for our ancestors.

Within living memory, women have accomplished the weekly wash without the aid of any but the most basic labour-saving devices and in some cases, without plumbed water. Depending on our age, our grandmothers, our mothers, or perhaps we ourselves, would have had to provide the family with clean clothes in this way.

For homes that lacked an indoor tap, the first task was to fetch the water. Although some households had their own pump or well outside, for most, this meant a walk to a source of water in the settlement where they lived. Pumping water, or winding the well bucket, was in itself a strenuous activity. A wooden bucket full of water might weigh as much as 4 stone (approximately 25kg). These heavy buckets, slopping water, then had to be carried home by hand or on a yoke. Alternatively, some women carried a bucket on their head, perhaps with a straw circlet to aid balance. Several trips to the village well might be needed to provide enough water for the laundry. Another option for our more distant ancestors, was to take the clothing to the river and wash it there. This made wash day a social occasion, as it was possible to gossip with neighbours engaged in the same task. The disadvantage of river water was that it was cold. For this reason, many women preferred to take the water home where it could be heated in a cauldron over the fire, or in a copper designed for the purpose.

Some wells in towns provided nearby washing blocks, where clothes could be pounded with stones or laundry bats. The laundry bat, also known as a battledore or beetle, was similar in shape to a cricket bat and the sport may well owe its origins to young lads borrowing their mothers' laundry bats and using them to hit a ball. Another way to break up the linen fibres and aid cleaning was to put the clothes in a tub of water and stamp up and down on them vigorously.

The following memories of wash day come from the 1950s:

After mother had got the fire alight we had to get water from the well and put into the boiler. She would wash the white shirts and sheets and other white items first and often used Reckitt's Blue to get the whites looking whiter. Before washing the shirts, she would scrub the collars to get them clean using a scrubbing board and put soap on the collars and brush them. After the whites were done and hung on the line she would start washing the other items. I know she washed the woollens and nylon things separately in a plastic bowl and I think at times she used soap flakes. There was also a mangle in the wash house and I would often hold on to the end of the sheet for her so she could put them through the wringer. We had a bowl underneath the mangle to catch the water that would be wrung out and then we used the water that was left to water the garden. We had a long clothes line and it would usually be full of sheets and pillow cases, which I would watch billowing in the breeze on a Monday morning. When the sheets were dry she would hang all the other clothes on the line and on a nice day it never took long to dry them.[1]

Even with the equipment available by the late 1960s, doing the weekly wash required the constant attention of the housewife:

For washing, mum had a twin tub with a mangle attached. She also had a cylindrical spin dryer with a rubber inner 'lid' that was supposed to stop clothes getting tangled in the works but wasn't always successful. This appliance would career over the floor as it spun the clothes violently. It had a spout near the bottom out of which came the water that had been dislodged. You had to put a washing-up bowl under the spout to catch the water. This required careful supervision as the cylinder could jerk round of its own accord, so that the spout was no longer over the bowl.[2]

If this seems alien to our twenty-first-century selves, how much more so the laundry practices of still-earlier generations. Before the development of washing powders, natural substances were used to aid cleansing; these had the advantage of being free. Lye was made in a lye-dropper, a large bucket-like receptacle with holes in the bottom. Ash was put in the tub, on top of layers of large stones and straw. Water was then dripped through the layers over a period of several days. Additional ingredients of lye might be guano or urine. Clothing that was to be steeped in lye would be layered in a buck, or bucking tub (a larger version of a bucket), which had a tap at the bottom. Lye would then be poured over the clothes and let out at the bottom as it drained through. Soap was made from animal fat, garnered when livestock was slaughtered. In seventeenth-century England, soap was subjected to a monopoly and its commercial manufacture was restricted to within a mile of London or Bristol. It was also heavily taxed.

If bleach was required, stale urine or animal dung was used. The urine would have been stored for two or three weeks in a bucking tub. As it also had many other uses, urine was a valuable commodity and some settlements had a communal urine barrel. The ammonia in the urine acted as a bleach. Sunlight was another valuable bleaching tool and the washing would be laid out in the sun, on the bleaching ground, to help it to whiten. Stubborn stains might be removed using vinegar, fuller's earth or bran.

Washing machines or 'agitators' began to find their way into more homes by the end of the nineteenth century. Other aids to washing included the ridged washing board, which might be wooden, or later glass. This provided a surface against which the clothing could be rubbed. Clothes could also be pounded with a 'dolly', a long pole with tripod-like 'legs' at the bottom. These legs were later replaced by a zinc cup at the base of the pole.

Once clean, the worst of the water would be wrung out. Two people would grasp each end of the garment and twist in opposing directions. Clothes might also be wrung out using a wringing post, or a convenient sapling. This could be accomplished by one person, as the shirt or sheet was looped round the post and then twisted on itself. Box mangles date back to the seventeenth century but these would have been too expensive for all but the most affluent families. Early models consisted of a large box of stones, which rested on rollers that had the clothes wound round them. The weight of the box squeezed out the water. Mangles found their way into many nineteenth-century households and it was often the job of small children to turn the handle of the mangle, so that moisture could be removed from the clothes. Mangles were also the source of many squashed fingers, as garments were fed in between the wooden rollers.

Crowded cottages, the smoky and smut-filled atmosphere, as well as the need to access the fire for activities such as cooking, meant that housewives were reluctant to dry the clothes in front of hearth. Doing so not only created the possible hazard of the clothing catching fire but the resulting dampness aggravated chest complaints. Ideally, clothing would be dried outside, often by draping it over a hedge. Primitive pegs were in use in the 1600s, although the 'line' might be a thin wooden pole balanced between two supports, rather than a rope. Once the clothes were dry enough for a final airing, they might be brought inside. By the late nineteenth century, many households had a wooden dryer, usually consisting of four parallel poles, that was suspended from the ceiling and could be let down on a pulley; alternatively, wooden clothes horses were used.

Ironing was not something that many ordinary housewives would have considered necessary. Those working as domestic servants for middle-class households would have used heavy, solid flat-irons, or sadirons. These were heated by the fire and came in different weights, so that lighter ones could be used for more delicate fabrics. At least two irons were needed as they lost heat very quickly, so one would be warming whist another was in use. Alternatively, box irons filled with hot coals or charcoal might be used and these kept warm for longer. The art of starching came from the Low Countries in the sixteenth century. Several methods of making starch evolved, including boiling horses' hooves, or using quickly boiled wheat, potatoes or rice, but starch was probably not used by poorer households. Proprietary starches were available from the end of the nineteenth century.

More recollections from the 1950s and 1960s:

After the washing was dried it was time for mum to do the ironing. This she did with a flat iron which was put on the range or electric stove if the range was not lit. She had two, so she could be heating one while she was using the other to iron. She had a thick cloth which went around the handle so she did not get burnt. She did not have an ironing board but ironed on the kitchen table, after removing the oilcloth and putting a thick ironing blanket and sheet on it. She had a large sleeve board that she used to do items which could not be ironed flat. After some time mum managed to get herself a Morphy Richards electric dry iron (we had not heard of steam irons). The flat did not have many electric plugs in the 1950s, as there were not many electrical devices to be had. So when mum had her electric iron it was plugged into the light socket, which meant that she could only do the ironing in the daytime.

I had an ironing board which was made out of wood and also a dry iron which rested on a piece of asbestos, when this wore out we bought another piece from the hardware shop and replaced it. No danger was attached to this in the mid-1960s.

Mum had cast iron irons heated on the stove. The heat of the iron was tested by spitting on it: if the spit jumped off as soon as it hit the iron, it was too hot! It was about right for cottons when it sizzled and disappeared straight away.[3]

'Doing the washing' was heavy work and the steamy atmosphere did not add to the attraction of the task. Whereas the lady of the house might indulge in a little baking, or even light dusting, if she could afford servants, the laundry was one of the first tasks that would be delegated. In larger households the lady's maid might be responsible for the more skilled tasks, such as wielding the goffering iron, used for maintaining frills, ruffs or pleats, or cleaning lace collars and cuffs, perhaps by rubbing them with bread. Taking in laundry was a way of poor women eking out a living. Commercial laundries, later 'launderettes', were, by the mid-twentieth century, used by many families for a least some of the wash. Perhaps this was because the practicalities of washing bedding in a small house, when they didn't own a washing machine, necessitated this:

> All the bed linen was white and went to the laundry every week. The local laundry man called on a Wednesday. Mum had a laundry book, issued by the company, which she filled in in duplicate each week, one copy going with the laundry and one copy for her to keep and then she checked it back the next week.[4]

The way in which one did the laundry helped to define one's place in the world. In the days of communal washing, those who were not present each week were regarded as wealthy. The implication being that they had several spare sets of linen and therefore it was not so imperative to wash every Monday. More recently, white washing on the line, or white net curtains at the windows were a mark of housewifely excellence; no one wished to be ridiculed for whites that were less than white.

Chapter 19

Textile Workers

Occupations associated with the textile industry are often perceived as being 'women's work'. After all, the very word 'spinster' means 'one who spins'. Prior to the Industrial Revolution, spinning and weaving were principally home industries, carried out by both men and women. Most housewives would spin and weave to produce sufficient cloth for the needs of their household, some producing a surplus for sale. As more household tasks were outsourced, including those associated with cloth production, commercial manufacture took over.

The new machinery of the late eighteenth and early nineteenth centuries sped up the process and took production from the home to increasingly large factories or mills. As one new invention increased the spinners' speed, so another was required to enable the weavers to keep up and vice versa. Apparatus such as Kay's Flying Shuttle, the Spinning Jenny, Crompton's Mule and looms by Cartwright and Jacquard, all contributed to the mechanisation of the textile industry.

Working with the machinery required dexterity, so women and children were preferred as employees. The nineteenth-century Factory Acts limited the employment of children. The 1833 Act banned those under the age of 9 from working in the mills and restricted the hours for 10- to 13-year-olds to forty-eight hours per week. By 1847, legislation reduced the maximum number of daily hours, for women and those under 18, to ten. In mid-nineteenth-century Britain, only agriculture and domestic service employed more individuals than the cotton mills. In the nineteenth century, Lancashire mills produced about 80 per cent of England's cotton.

The years 1861–1865 saw what was known as the Cotton Famine, or the Cotton Panic. This depression in the cotton industry was partly due to shrinking world markets and overproduction in preceding years but was exacerbated by the American Civil War, which had a huge impact on the cotton industry, as it disrupted the imports of raw cotton and made life very precarious for the British workforce. Nonetheless, nearly ½ million people were still employed by the Lancashire cotton industry in 1911, with women comprising more than half the mills' workforce.

Chapter 1, 'A Stitch in Time', describes the making of clothes in the domestic context; now it is time to focus on commercial production. The textiles that were manufactured ranged from blankets and woollen cloth, such as worsteds, to linens, cottons and silks. There were several roles for women within the textile industry. In the cotton mills, bales of raw cotton would be washed and carded and then wound on to a sliver. The slivers were drawn out into even strands. Two more machines, a slubbing frame and a roving frame, twisted and drew the strands out still further, before they were wound onto a bobbin ready for spinning.

Woolcombing, or carding raw wool, often required a man's strength, depending on the type of fleece but might also be undertaken by women. The fleeces would require cleaning first and this was often done in hot, steamy conditions. Mule-spinning was highly skilled and normally undertaken by men but women might have assisted, usually by joining broken threads. In 1825, the process of wet-spinning was introduced in Leeds flax mills, mainly employing young girls.

In the days before health and safety legislation, there were many health hazards associated with working with textiles. Woolcombing affected the lungs, as dust fibres would be inhaled. Byssinosis is a form of asthma that is sometimes referred to as 'brown lung disease'. It was prevalent among textile workers and was contracted when workers regularly inhaled unprocessed cotton, hemp, or flax fibres. It is thought that the condition is caused by bacteria that live on the plants. The condition was particularly likely if the work took place in a poorly ventilated area.

In 1831, Charles Thackrah wrote 'The Effects of the Principal Arts, Trades and Professions and of Civic States and Habits of Living on Health and Longevity'. Of weavers he said:

> Weavers have a confined atmosphere and though limbs are fully exercised, the trunk is kept comparatively fixed and the chest is not expanded. This stooping, however, is somewhat diminished by the mode of casting the shuttle with a string, instead of the hand. Digesting is imperfect, asthma and other afflictions of the chest are common. They complain of the smell from the oil-lamps.[1]

His book includes some case studies, so we can learn that:

> S.J. aged 33 is a back minder (i.e. a person placed at the back of the roving machines). She has been fifteen years in the flax mills. She was healthy when she entered but was soon attacked with a cough and vomiting, which have increased and continue. The cough, she says, comes on in paroxysms, like the whooping cough. The matter she expectorates is frothy and sometimes purulent. Her respirations is habitually oppressed, but occasionally so much worse, especially in winter, that it is with difficulty she can walk from the mill to her lodging, a quarter of a mile distant, She is tall, stoops much and is of a very sickly appearance. Her digestive organs are impaired. She complains of a pain across the base of the chest, with occasional but great swelling at the pit of the stomach.[2]

When the clothing was discarded, women might still be working with the rags, or 'shoddy', as it was known. This was turned into a poor-quality cloth. Rag sorting was one of the lowliest tasks and often undertaken by women who were nearing destitution. A description of the rag-sorting room at Messrs Blakely's mill on the outskirts of Dewsbury appeared in the *Morning Chronicle* in 1849.[3] This was later published in Henry Mayhew's *London Labour and the London Poor*.[4] It provides an evocative account of the process and conditions in which the women were working:

> Under the rag ware-room was the sorting and picking area. Here the bales are opened and their contents piled in close, poverty-smelling masses upon the floor. The operatives were entirely women. They sat upon low stools, or half sunk and half enthroned amid heaps of filthy goods, busily employed in arranging them according to the colour and quality ... carefully ripping out every particle of cotton which they could detect. Piles of rags of different sorts, dozens of feet high, were the obvious fruits of their labour. All the women ... looked squalid and dirty enough, but all of them were chattering, and several singing, over their noisome labour. The atmosphere of the room was close and oppressive; and although I perceived no particularly offensive smell, we could not help being sensible to the presence of a choky, mildew sort of odour – a hot, moist exhalation – arising from the sodden smouldering piles as the workwomen tossed armfuls of rags from one heap to another. In this mill, as at this species of work – the lowest and foulest which any phase of the factory system can show – I found, for the first time, labouring as regular mill hands, Irish women.

At this date, it is likely that the Irish women were those fleeing the Irish famine that resulted from the failure of the potato crop.

These workers were affected by the dirt, smell and choking dust, which irritated the lungs and caused dry throats. Breathing difficulties, including asthma, and eye problems such as 'pink eye' were all associated with working as a rag sorter. The woollen rags frequently harboured fleas and other pests. There are accounts of dead rats and even a dead baby being found among the bundles of rags that had been salvaged. Skin conditions and infections were common if the skin was already broken. The most severe consequence of rag sorting was pulmonary anthrax contracted from inhalation of the dust; this complaint was even more common among wool sorters. Even as late as 1903, the *Derby Daily Telegraph* reported a rag-sorter's death from anthrax, yet claimed that no blame was attached to anybody.[5]

The working conditions in the textile industry were notoriously poor, even in the context of the nineteenth century. Sadly, in some parts of the world, conditions are little better today for those who work to produce our clothing.

Ada Fieldhouse's Story

Ada Fieldhouse was born on 5 May 1885, in the iconic textile community of Saltaire, near Bradford in West Yorkshire. Saltaire had been founded in 1853 by industrialist Titus Salt, later Sir Titus Salt, whose vision was to create an ideal textile mill and surroundings. He believed that better accommodation and working conditions and a contented workforce could only benefit his business. This meant that Ada and other members of her family, who also worked in the mill, would have experienced a better working and living environment than those who were employed in mills elsewhere.

Ada was the sixth of seven children of James and Mary Ann Fieldhouse née Shepherd, although three of her older siblings had died in infancy. In 1891, the family were living at 22 Constance Street. Ada's 12-year-old brother was a spinning doffer, removing the full bobbins from the spinning frames and replacing them with empty ones; her older sister was a twister and her father was an overlooker in the carding department.

A newspaper report in 1892 reveals that an Ada Fieldhouse took the part of Boy Blue in a pantomime performed by children at the Theatre Royal. This may be our Ada. The family's address in 1901 was 24 Constance Street, this could be the renumbering of their previous home. The homes in Constance Street reflect Titus Salt's ethos and are solid-looking brick houses, with attractive arched windows and five rooms. Many working-class families of six would not have been able to afford to live in such a spacious home. At the age of 15, Ada was working at the mill as a spinner, alongside her older brother, a comb minder and her father, a cashmere card cleaner. Her younger brother had not gone into the mill but was apprenticed to a printer.

A photograph of Saltaire Congregational Sunday School Young Ladies' Class, taken in 1906, includes Ada. At the end of that year Ada performed in the Congregational Church's Concert and acted as a 'tray holder'. In May 1907, she was a waitress for the church's jubilee celebrations. This seemingly pleasant existence for a young mill worker was to end as events took a tragic turn. On Friday, 9 August of 1907 Ada was, as usual, working as a spinner at Saltaire Mills. The machine had been stopped for cleaning and Ada failed to hear the signal that it was to restart, although the girls close to her had heard it. Had years of working in the noisy mill environment perhaps affected Ada's hearing? As a consequence, Ada did not stand clear of the machine as it restarted and her right arm was torn out of the shoulder. She was rushed to hospital and doctors were able to save her life but not her arm.

The community rallied round and the next month a benefit concert was held in the Congregational Church Schoolroom. Ada was described as a member of the Congregational Young People's Meeting. The entertainment was not just provided by her own church members, as the Baptists' Girls Own Band also took part.

There was also a bun- and jelly-eating competition. Eight pounds was raised for Ada, which might have been equivalent to three months' wages.

Ada continued to be a member of the Congregational Church and lived at 24 Constance Street with her family. In 1911, she was described as a stocking knitter who was working on her own account from home. This must surely have been difficult with one arm. After the death of her father, Ada, her mother and her older sister Annie went to live at 23 Shirley Street in Saltaire. By this time, Ada was running a draper's shop from home as well as knitting stockings. Again, the family were benefiting from Saltaire's superior accommodation, which did not resemble typical working-class Victorian terraced housing.

In 1929, a Miss Fieldhouse of the City Mission spoke to the Congregational Church's Young People's Fellowship about her services among the poor of the city. Could this have been Ada, or perhaps her older sister, Annie?

The two sisters remained living at Shirley Street, with Ada running the draper's and haberdashery, until Annie's death in December 1943. Shortly after this, Ada moved to be near her brother, Ernest, who was living in Morecombe and, having given up his work as a printer, was the proprietor of the roundabout in the Winter Gardens' fairground. When he died, in 1950, his effects were left to his widow, another Annie and to Ada.

Ada died on 22 July 1965 and was described as being of 113 Alexandra Road, Morecombe at the time. Ernest's widow, Annie, attended the funeral and she herself died the following week. Although Ada was employed by the textile mill for fewer than ten years, her life was shaped by the consequences of that work.

Chapter 20

Buttony

As mentioned previously, particularly in rural areas, many women took advantage of the flexibility of piece work within the home, with different parts of the country being noted for different types of piece work. In Dorset, in the south-west of the country, it was wound-thread button-making, or buttony, that was the most popular way for women to earn money at home. Further north, in the towns of Macclesfield in Cheshire and Leek in Staffordshire, it was silk button-making.

Buttons have been used on clothing for thousands of years, but the craft of Dorset button-making dates back to the late 1600s, when Abraham Case began to produce these unique buttons. Fashions were changing and buttons were replacing lacing as the main method of fastening clothing. At this time, buttons were becoming more decorative, rather than just being functional. Case had fought in Europe during the Thirty Years War and was aware of the newly popular continental styles. Another, unverified, story is that he observed soldiers creating makeshift buttons using wire and linen while on the battlefield.

The first buttons produced by Case were created by using linen to cover small rings of horn from Dorset Horn sheep. The fabric was then stitched over to give the button a conical shape or 'High-Top'. Dorset Knobs were a similar type of raised button. The numbers involved in button-making grew rapidly and soon several thousand workers, predominantly women, were working from home. A 1699 Act of Parliament might have been problematic for the trade as it forbade the making of buttons from 'cloth, serge, drugget, or other stuffs'. The Dorset button-makers ignored this directive, even though it was still on the statute books until 1867.

In the middle of the eighteenth century, a new technique was developed. A circle of wire was created by twisting it on a spindle and soldering the ends. The wire was imported in large rolls from Birmingham. It was often the role of small children to work as winders and dippers for this part of the process. At the height of production, children were recruited from the local workhouses for these tasks. Stringers would wind wool round the ring and weave it across the circle of wire in a number of traditional patterns. These include Crosswheels, Ten-spoke Yarrels, Honeycomb Crosswheels and Spangles. Blandford Cartwheels utilised the skills of the Dorset lace makers and were made using white linen thread. Mitres and Birds' Eyes used a slightly different technique, with the ring being created from a small rolled-up piece of fabric.

As the trade flourished, several towns established depots where the buttons were collected from the home workers ready for redistribution. Each Friday, or 'Button Day', hundreds of women would walk to their nearest depot to hand in their finished buttons and collect their pay and the raw materials for the following week. A sales office was opened in London, and Abraham's grandson, Peter Case, set up an export business for the buttons, with a base in Liverpool that generated a turnover of several thousand pounds. He also developed a rustproof alloy for the wire rings. The buttons were popular for shirts and underclothing as they were easily washed.

Any buttons that had become soiled in transit were boiled in a linen bag in order to clean them without damage. The completed buttons were sewn onto sheets of card ready for sale. Different quality buttons were arranged on different coloured card, with pink being reserved for the best quality. Lesser buttons were put on navy card and those of the poorest quality on yellow. Buttons intended for the domestic market, rather than export, were sewn onto black card. Children were used to sort buttons and mount them on the cards.

A dozen buttons could sell for between 8d and 3s. Proficient buttoners might reach an output of a gross (144) a day, which would earn them perhaps as much as 3s 6d, three times the wage of a farm labourer.

By the nineteenth century, inventors were working on button-making machines. In 1825, a machine for making cloth and thread buttons was devised by Benjamin Saunders. This was followed by John Aston's machine. When Aston's 'button-press', for making metal buttons, was exhibited at the Great Exhibition of 1851, the hand-made button industry rapidly declined. Machine button-making moved to the factories of the Midlands' industrial towns. Many of the redundant home workers had been those whose families were living close to the poverty line and the loss of this income was catastrophic. The resulting economic distress led many of the former workers to emigrate. It is thought that 350 left the Dorset town of Sherborne alone, bound for America and Australia.

Another area noted for its button-making was Macclesfield in Cheshire, a traditional silk-weaving town that was much further north than Dorset. The technique they employed was slightly different, with fine threads, such as silk or mohair, being wrapped and woven over a wooden base. Like the button-makers of Dorset, most of the Macclesfield buttons were made by female home workers. Their 'Death's Head' button design is still used for official clerical or legal dress. These were sometimes known as Passementerie Buttons, or Leek Buttons, named after another centre of production, Leek in Staffordshire.

There are instances of early seventeenth-century wills and inventories listing button-making materials and the Macclesfield trade was well established by this time. As early as 1709, silk button-making provided employment for several thousand button-makers and support trades, such as dyers. It is thought that home working such as this increased the family's income by 50 per cent. The Mottershead family were predominant in the silk button-making trade and in 1743, Charles Row built a button mill. The silk came from Spitalfields in London, where there was a skilled Huguenot workforce. This northern button trade also made use of pauper children. The buttons were often sold by peddlers or chapmen, but there were merchants as far away as London, Scotland and Ireland, distributing and exporting silk buttons. The trade here was in decline by the end of the eighteenth century.

Chapter 21

Votes for Women: The Fight for Female Suffrage

Although campaigning for the right to vote might not be considered an occupation, or a domestic task, there were women who spent many hours working towards a universal franchise. Organisations such as the Women's Social and Political Union had both paid and voluntary staff, meaning that the activities of the suffragists and suffragettes did constitute work. Suffragists were all those who took part in the movements. Suffragette was a term that was coined by a *Daily Mail* reporter in 1906 and was intended to be derisory, but the women embraced the name. 'Suffragette' is normally associated with the more militant wing of the movement.

It is important to remember that most of our great-grandmothers and perhaps our grandmothers, were born into a world where women were disenfranchised. Of course, in many countries, a century ago, working-class men had not long had the right to vote, but as the First World War came to a close, many English-speaking women did not hold equal voting rights with men. In some of these countries, from the mid-nineteenth century, there had been limited opportunities for women to vote in local elections if they owned substantial property but universal franchise did not begin to arrive until the 1890s. The right to stand for parliament often lagged behind gaining the vote.

New Zealand was the most enlightened, extending voting rights to women as early as 1893, thus becoming the world leader. There, the Women's Christian Temperance Union (WCTU) leader, Kate Sheppard, was a prime mover in the suffrage campaign. The names and addresses of the 24,000 New Zealand signatories to the 1893 suffrage petition can be searched at **https://nzhistory.govt.nz/politics/womens-suffrage**. This site also gives a great deal of background information. The names of those who signed the petitions of 1892 and 1893 have also been indexed on Findmypast.

Although South Australia granted women the vote comparatively early, in 1894, it was 1902 before this was nationwide and another sixty years after that before the right was extended to the Indigenous population, both male and female. Petitioning was a common tactic among the Australian suffragists and some of the petitions are searchable online. For example, the 1891 Victorian Women's petition can be found at **www.parliament.vic.gov.au/about/history-and-heritage/people-who-shaped-parliament/women-suffrage-search/**.

Canada introduced votes for women on a province by province basis, beginning in Ontario in 1884. Those in Quebec had to wait until 1940 and First Nations' women were not able to vote until 1960. Nellie McClung, one of the founders of the Political Equality League, was prominent in the Canadian campaign, which was boosted by a visit by Mrs Pankhurst, from England, in 1911, although some Canadian suffragists resented being told what to do by a foreigner.

The United States also extended the franchise to women in a piecemeal manner, with individual states gradually granting the right to vote in different categories of election. Elizabeth Cady Stanton, Susan B. Anthony and Lucy Stone spearheaded the American campaign. In the early years of the twentieth century, the National Women's Party, led by Alice Paul, began picketing the White House and Lafayette Park. Many of the campaigners were jailed, leading to hunger strikes and forced feeding. The American position was rationalised in 1920 but it was not until the Civil Rights Movement of the 1960s that Black women in some southern states were actually able to exercise their democratic rights.

A racial divide was also evident in South Africa, with European and Asian women gaining the vote in 1930 but those of other races having to wait until 1994. In South Africa, it was the Women's Christian Temperance Union that was the vehicle for suffragist activity.

In Ireland, the Dublin Women's Suffrage Association was formed, by Anna Haslam, as early as 1847. Their first petition to parliament, in 1866, was signed by just twenty-five women. The campaign for votes for women was intertwined with the fight for Home Rule and the two movements sat uneasily alongside each other. The suffragists' campaign gained renewed vigour in 1908, when Hannah and Francis Sheehy-Skeffington and Margaret Cousins founded the Irish Women's Franchise League (IWFL), whose aim was to enfranchise women within Home Rule. The partition of Ireland meant that women from the age of 21 were given the vote in the Republic in 1922, whereas those north of the border had to wait until 1928.

Although there had been earlier examples of some British women voting in local elections and the Isle of Man had given property-owning women the vote in 1881, in Britain, it was the active role of women during the First World War, aided by the rise of the Labour movement, that proved to be the final catalyst, leading to women aged 30 and over, being able to vote from 1918. The reason for the age disparity was because, owing to the loss of so many men in the war, if the minimum age had been set lower, female voters would have significantly outnumbered the men and this was seen as unacceptable. By 1928, British women enjoyed equal voting rights with men.

In a similar manner to other nations, there were two distinct strands to the British Woman's Rights Movement: those who wanted to bring about change through peaceful, legal campaigning and those who were willing to take more militant action. Despite their common cause, the two wings of the movement were often at odds with each other. The radical suffragettes were blamed by their more peaceful sisters for giving the movement a bad name and bringing the cause into disrepute. On the other hand, the militants felt that the law-abiding approach was ineffective.

It is important to acknowledge that, in all countries, there were enlightened men who were supportive of the fight for women's suffrage and equally, there were women who despised their 'unladylike' sisters for not accepting their position in life. Indeed, without their male supporters, the women would have had a much more difficult time, as they sought to bring about change. Particularly in the early days, activists were often middle-class, educated women, who could present their case articulately, but the movement quickly attracted women of all classes.

In 1866, 1,500 individuals put their names to a petition that was presented to the House of Commons by John Stuart Mill. The original petition does not survive but a printed pamphlet listing the signatories' names and addresses was circulated. A transcript of a surviving pamphlet has been made and can be viewed at www.parliament.uk/globalassets/documents/parliamentary-archives/1866SuffragePetitionNamesWebJune16.pdf. It is searchable on Findmypast.

The British campaign really gained momentum in 1897, when the National Union of Women's Suffrage Societies (NUWSS) was formed, bringing together seventeen smaller groups. To begin with, their activities were primarily confined to publishing pamphlets and writing letters to MPs. By 1907, protest marches had become part of their toolkit. In the meantime, some women became frustrated with the lack of progress and in 1903, the break-away movement, The Women's Social and Political Union (WSPU), was formed under Emmeline Pankhurst. Their methods were more proactive and they were willing to break the law. They began accosting politicians and heckling at hustings and other political meetings. Some went further and several arson attacks were attributed to the suffragettes.

Many of the women had their health impaired by periods in prison. They frequently went on hunger strike and as a consequence, were force-fed. This policy led to protests and in 1913, the Prisoners' Temporary Discharge for Ill-health Act, also known as the 'Cat and Mouse' Act, was passed. This meant that women on hunger strike were released, only to be re-arrested when they were no longer weak from the lack of food.

Thirteen different suffragette newspaper titles dating from 1894–1945 can be viewed on Findmypast, including *The Suffragette* (later renamed *Britannia*), which was edited by Christabel Pankhurst. Although you can search *The Suffragette* for names using Findmypast's Suffragette collection link, some of the other publications are browse-only records; there is no name search. The Suffragette Collection also contains images of other relevant documents. *The Suffragette* is also available and searchable on the British Newspaper Archive (BNA).

A list of suffragettes who were arrested between 1906 and 1914 is held at TNA in class HO45 and can be view at Ancestry. TNA also has details of suffragettes' complaints about their treatment in prison, in class HO144. Local newspapers are a good source of information about suffragette and suffragist activity in your ancestral area. Perhaps family members would have attended a political meeting, or a march.

In 1911, many suffragettes attempted to avoid completing the census. Slogans such as 'No Vote, No Census' were scrawled across the forms and groups of women spent the night in public places, in an effort to elude the enumerator. Militant suffragism took a blow when Emily Davison was killed as she threw herself under the king's horse at the Derby, in 1913. When war broke out the following year, there was a tacit agreement to suspend the campaign for the vote for the duration of the hostilities. Instead, the WSPU focused on recruiting women for vital roles that had been left vacant by men on active service. About 2 million women were employed in this way during the First World War. This made a significant contribution towards women proving their worth in occupations that were traditionally associated with men and strengthened their argument that they should have equal voting rights.

So what impact would the suffragists' fight have had on our ancestors? To begin with, the differences between the rights of men and women are indicative of how women were viewed in general. It was genuinely believed, by many, that women lacked the intellectual capacity to vote. It is important to stress that we are now viewing this situation with hindsight and while twenty-first-century society might find the disparity between the sexes deplorable, at the time, most men and indeed many women, would have accepted the status quo and would have had no aspirations to bring about change. Others, though, railed against this discrimination and were willing to campaign for equality. It is a sobering thought to realise that the concept of female voters is still a very new one in some parts of the world.

Chapter 22

Teaching and Learning

In order to teach, women had themselves to have been educated and educational opportunities for women were limited until the 1900s, with inequalities in curriculum and societal expectations remaining for most of the twentieth century. Academic education for women was regarded as unnecessary at best and dangerous at worst. What women needed, according to the prevailing view, were the skills required to run a household and raise children. Women's brains were regarded as inferior and incapable of grasping intellectual concepts, with education for women being considered by many to be positively harmful and likely to lead to vice. Yet, in the centuries before compulsory schooling, much of what children learned was from their mothers, not their fathers – although the focus was on practical skills, not book learning.

The attitude to women's education is exemplified by this memory from a woman, who left school at 18, in the 1960s:

> It was not so common for people to go to university in those days and my parents were not very enthusiastic. When I came back from my summer job of waitressing in a hotel, just three weeks before going to university and said how much I had enjoyed it, my mother asked if I really wanted to go to university, because it would save them a lot of expense if I didn't go and I 'would probably get married anyway'.[1]

In medieval times, despite women founding schools and colleges, they were not educated at them. In order to gain an education, a woman had little option but to enter a convent and take religious orders. The Humanist Movement of the early 1500s, followed by the Protestant Reformation, had their part to play in increasing literacy for both women and men. With the Reformation came church services and Bibles in English. The Puritans, in particular, were anxious that women could read the Bible, in order to rear suitably pious children. Not all Protestant reformers were agreed on the matter of education for women, however; Martin Luther was very much in favour, while Presbyterian, John Knox, was a vehement opponent.

In the sixteenth and seventeenth centuries, literate women were invariably from the more affluent sections of society. On the subject of schooling for girls, in 1561, Richard Mulcaster, cited Queen Elizabeth as a positive example of an educated women and wrote: 'Our country doth allow it; our duty doth enforce it, their aptness calls for it; their excellency commands it.'[2] This enlightened view was rare and Mulcaster himself did not envisage that women's education would encompass geometry, science, medicine, rhetoric or law.

The rise of the new merchant class at this time was accompanied by an increase in the number of schools for boys, who were now more likely to be taught by schoolmasters, rather than members of the clergy. Although formal schooling was still emphatically the preserve of males, it became desirable for middle- and upper-class women to be literate and numerate, in order to run their households, but girls were habitually taught at home.

By the 1700s, there was an interest in promoting education for women, mostly among the wealthier sections of society. In the mid-eighteenth century, the Blue Stockings Society, was founded by Elizabeth Montagu and Elizabeth Vesey. This was a loose association of like-minded individuals. Society hostesses would arrange meetings of this informal group, who would take tea and discuss, literature, politics and the arts. Men were also invited to attend these gatherings.

Particularly before the advent of compulsory education, becoming a governess was seen as a respectable job for an unmarried woman. These women, who were often the daughters of professional men, required no formal training but merely passed on what they themselves had been taught. As their pupils were usually girls, or very young boys, no academic rigour was expected. For girls, much importance was placed on suitably feminine 'accomplishments', as well as the need to learn how to run a household, manage servants and behave in polite society. Apart from basic literacy, the emphasis was on needlework, painting, music, dancing, deportment and perhaps a little French.

The Governesses' Benevolent Institution was set up, in 1843, to assist governesses in 'illness, distress and old age'. In 1848, they founded Queen's College, London, to provide girls with a further education and to enable them to gain qualifications. It did, however, pander to the view that girls were suited to a different type of education from boys and did not attempt to emulate a typical male curriculum. In 1872, they also set up a home for retired governesses in Chislehurst, Kent.

Lower down the social scale, women often presided over dame schools. Frequently, these were little more than glorified child-minding arrangements, with the 'mistress' looking after children, of a variety of ages, in her own home, without imparting anything resembling a formal education. As has been pointed out in other chapters, 'schools' were set up, primarily for girls, that taught craft skills, such as lacemaking and straw plaiting but the education did not go beyond that craft.

By the mid-nineteenth century, women's literacy rates were on the rise. In 1840, only about 40 per cent of women could read and write but this would increase to 60 per cent in the following twenty years. Nonconformist Sunday schools, in particular, placed an emphasis on learning to read, giving both boys and girls great opportunities to acquire basic literacy, although there was less emphasis on the ability to write. Literary societies became popular and towns and villages opened reading rooms, where newspapers and books were made available. Educational lectures were provided, notably in the towns. In London, The Mechanics' Institute allowed women to attend its evening lectures from 1830.

The monitorial system was common in schools set up in the early nineteenth century, under the auspices of the National Society for Promoting the Education of the Poor in the Principles of the Established Church in England and Wales (National Schools) and the Nonconformist equivalent British and Foreign School Society (British Schools). Older children were taught by the teachers and then imparted this knowledge to younger children. The monitors might then go on to become teachers themselves.

The concept that teachers needed to be trained to teach, rather than just acquire subject knowledge, did not develop until well into the nineteenth century. In 1847, Lord Macaulay, in a speech to the House of Commons, described teachers as:

> The refuse of all other callings, discarded footmen, ruined pedlars, men who cannot work a sum in the rule of three, men who do not know whether the earth is a sphere or a cube, men who do not know whether Jerusalem is in Asia or America. And to such men, men to whom none of us would entrust the key of his cellar, we have entrusted the mind of the rising generation, and with the mind of the rising generation, the freedom, the happiness, the glory of our country.[3]

Women who taught would have been regarded with even greater disdain.

In 1873, the all-female college, Girton College, was founded at Cambridge by Barbara Bodichon and Emily Davies but it was 1948 before the college was fully integrated into the university. Frances Buss opened a school, with her mother, in Kentish Town in 1845. This was to become the North London Collegiate School for Ladies, which is recognised as the first school for girls to offer an academic education, similar to that which boys might receive. Nonetheless, in many schools, the gendered curriculum lasted until the end of the twentieth century, when boys still learned woodwork and metalwork, while girls did needlework and domestic science.

Prestigious girls' boarding schools such as Cheltenham Ladies' College and Roedean, founded in 1853 and 1885 respectively, were open to very few. In 1872, The Girls' Day School Trust was founded by Mrs Maria Grey, Miss Emily Shirreff, Miss Mary Gurney and Lady Stanley of Alderney. Records, from 1873–1950, of both staff and students of the schools set up under the trust are available on Ancestry.

Dorothea Beale, an associate of Frances Buss, became the principal of Cheltenham Ladies' College in 1858. She became aware of the lack of teacher training opportunities for women and, in 1876, opened St Hilda's College in Cheltenham, providing residential training. In 1892, she purchased property in Oxford, which became St Hilda's Hall of residence, allowing the women to benefit from a year at Oxford. By the late nineteenth century, universities began to accept women, although they were slower to award women degrees. The first to do so was London University in 1878. Oxford followed suit in 1920 but it was not until 1948 that women at Cambridge were able to graduate with a degree.

A significant change in educational opportunities for girls came with the introduction of compulsory education. By 1880, all 5- to 10-year-olds had to attend school. The school-leaving age rose steadily until it reached 14 in 1915 and 15 in 1947. Compared to boys, fewer girls were given the opportunity to stay on beyond the statutory school-leaving age. The attitude that education for girls was wasted, as they were destined for domestic duties, still prevailed well into the second half of the twentieth century.

The government formally set up the pupil-teacher system in 1846. Both boys and girls, as they neared the end of their own education, might take on the role of pupil teachers, combining the instruction of younger pupils with their own studies. This was only an option for those whose families did not expect or require them to work elsewhere, as training normally took five years, until the pupil teacher was 18. School inspectors examined pupil teachers each year, observing their teaching and judging their academic competence. Pupil teachers might continue as uncertified teachers, or they could take the Queen's Scholarship examination, after which successful candidates received a grant to enter a training college. Training was not essential to continue in the role. In the 1880s, pupil-teacher centres were set up to provide professional and academic training. Provision remained patchy and there was no national standard.

Concerns about teaching standards led to the government enquiry into state education, the Cross Commission, in 1888. Two years later, grants were awarded to provide day training centres. Balfour's Education Act of 1902 put the responsibility for education, including the training of teachers, in the hands of the newly created Local Education Authorities, leading to the foundation of many teacher training colleges. This effectively put an end to the pupil-teacher system.

Female teachers were overwhelmingly single; a married woman's place was seen as being at home. Although the Sex Disqualification Removal Act of 1919 made it easier, in theory, for women to train as teachers, the 'marriage bar' requiring all women to resign as soon as they married, remained in place until the Second World War, when married women, with no young children to care for, were encouraged to return to teaching to cover for male teachers who were in the forces. The ban was finally removed in 1944, although societal attitudes that disapproved of married women working, in any sphere, remained.

An appeal against the marriage bar, in 1925, by Mrs Ethel Florence Short, a Dorset schoolteacher, illustrates the attitudes of the time. The appeal court judge said:

> The duty of a married woman is primarily to look after her domestic concerns and it is impossible for her to do so and to effectively and satisfactorily act as a teacher at the same time ... It is unfair to the large number of young unmarried teachers seeking situations that the positions should be occupied by married women, who presumably have husbands capable of maintaining them.[4]

The move to establish a register for teachers, similar to that for doctors, began in the mid-nineteenth century but met with a great deal of opposition. A Teachers' Registration Council was finally set up in 1902. Apart from an hiatus from 1907–1911, the minutes of the council, up until it was disbanded in 1949 are at TNA. The Teaching Unions, which had been formed in the second half of the nineteenth century, objected to the proposed distinctions between teachers with different types of qualification, so the register, without those distinctions, did not begin until 1914. The register did include those currently teaching, some of whom had been in post for many years. The registration cards, detailing the career of registered teachers, are held by the Society of Genealogists and are available online at Findmypast. Some of these records are missing and not all teachers were registered.

Teaching was one of the first professions to be considered to be a respectable career for women. Into the 1970s, along with nursing and secretarial work, it was touted by schools, as most careers departments were reluctant to suggest more adventurous options for girls.

Chapter 23

Pottery Workers

The Potteries, the area around Stoke-on-Trent in Staffordshire, with its supplies of suitable clay and coal, was the ideal location for pottery-producing factories, or 'potbanks'. Some of the 180 potbanks were small concerns but others were the industry leaders, such as Royal Doulton and Wedgwood. One of the reasons why the potbanks in Stoke-on-Trent were so successful, is that they were swift to convert to using coal, rather than wood, as fuel for their iconic beehive, or bottle-shaped, kilns. Although the use of coal was more cost-effective, at a time when timber supplies were dwindling, there was a significant disadvantage to the use of coal. It had a devastating effect on the air quality in the area. The pollution was notorious and was hugely detrimental to the health of the workers and other residents.

The potbanks were producing such things as tableware, tiles, pipes, ornaments and sanitaryware. By the mid-eighteenth century, clay was being brought in from places as far away as Devon and Cornwall, in order to manufacture different types of product. Even after it became less important to have a local supply of clay, the Potteries remained the centre of the industry, probably because of the expertise of the workforce. There were, of course, also factories elsewhere; Doulton's in Lambeth, south London, for example, was employing about 300 women in the late nineteenth century.

It was an industry in which a female workforce played a significant part. In 1851, a third of all pottery workers were women or girls and this would increase to more than 50 per cent by the early twentieth century. As the raising of the school-leaving age deprived the factories of the youngest workers, women, as the cheapest alternative, were employed to replace them; there were still 30,000 women working in the pottery industry as late as 1977.[1] Inevitably, it was the male employees who were more likely to hold positions of authority and who commanded higher wages.

There was a wide variety of roles in the potbank, with women dominating in the later stages of the process, notably transferring the printed designs to the ceramics, decorating the ware and working in the warehouse. Women were employed in the potting shops, predominantly producing cups and saucers, or attaching spouts and handles. They might also be involved in the creation of plates and saucers by pressing clay into moulds. Some of the tasks were more prestigious than others, with those who were involved in the preparation of the clay at the 'dirty end' being looked down upon by those such as the painters and gilders.

The lack of machinery involved in the process meant that the potbanks were not legally classified as factories until the 1860s, so they were exempt from factory legislation, including regulations regarding the age of employees and permitted working hours. The first investigation into the use of child labour in the potteries was carried out by Samuel Scriven in 1840. His report followed a survey of 173 potteries, looking specifically at working conditions and the treatment of children, many of whom were female.[2] At this time, much of the work, including making, decorating and firing the ware, was paid on a piece-work basis. In order to produce as much as possible, the potters employed children, aged between 8 and 14 as assistants. As it was the individual workers, not the factory, that hired the children, the factories were not responsible for the pay or conditions in which the children worked. It was not until they reached the age of about 13 or 14 that children might be taken on by the factory as apprentices.

In 1860, Dr Greenhow, investigating the high preponderance of lung disease in the Potteries, found that those who lived and worked there were twice as likely to die from pulmonary conditions than those in 'healthy districts'. Women employed in dipping and printing were at greatest risk. Greenhow stated that women and girls were employed as gilders, burnishers and scourers, with the scourers being 'the most pernicious branch of the manufacture'.[3] As the dusty factories were often only swept weekly, this is hardly surprising.

Scriven had reported:

When china ware is to be fired, it is first placed in coarse earthen vessels called 'saggers'; these contain a quantity of finely pulverized flint; this during the firing, attaches itself strongly to the china; some two, three, or more young women are employed to scour it off with sand paper and brushes; the particles float abundantly in the atmosphere of the rooms and cover their persons.[4]

Several workers provided testimonies that appear in Scriven's report, the text of which appears on the website www.thepotteries.org/history/scriven.htm. Evidence from 33-year-old Fanny Wood reads as follows:

I have been a scourer seven years; always with Mr Daniel; have two rooms opening into each other; one man and three women are employed here, and no children; we get our ware from the biscuit-oven, and have to scour it; it then goes to the dipping-house. The work does not agree with us very well, because it is so dusty it makes one short of breath; everyone that works in this place suffers more or less with coughs, and we are all stuffed up; we have known a great many deaths from it; we come at seven, leave at six; are paid by the oven; that is like being paid by the piece, and average 8 shillings per week. William Benley, who stands by me, has been seventeen years in the place, and he knows five women who have died from it, and numbers that have been obliged to leave it; he now says he couldn't enumerate the number, there have been so many.[5]

Some of the women, mostly those in supervisory roles, told Scriven that they observed no detrimental effects on their health. Some of the youngest girls were of the opinion that conditions were good and that work in the potbanks was preferable to working elsewhere. Ann Dishley, aged 9, said:

> I have been a painter twelve months last Martinmas. There are eight little girls work in the same room with me. Mary Worrelow looks after us; we all come to work at six o'clock in the morning, and go home at six, some go home to dinner; an hour is allowed us for dinner, and half an hour for breakfast. I can read very well, but can't write; I go to Bethesda Sunday-school, and went two years to day-school; they didn't teach me to write. Ann Dishley is very good to us, she never flogs us, or master either; she is my mother. We get holidays, altogether perhaps a month.[6]

Others, however, like Fanny, complained about the conditions and reported that they suffered from lung and other complaints, as a result of their work. Nineteen-year-old Ann Baker, who worked in the Ridgeway factory, told Scriven:

> I have worked three years in these works, first in the biscuit warehouse, then in the dipping-house; my duty is to scrape the uneven dipping off the ware when dry; the occupation is a very unhealthy one. I cannot eat my food as I used to do; it affects my chest very much, makes me cough; I have a tightness on my chest; standing all day does not hurt me.[7]

In 1862, Francis Longe added to Scriven's evidence in a report to the Children's Employment Commission, which covered child labour in several industries. He observed:

> I often see a father of a family, a plate or saucer maker, have with him several of his children, girls as well as boys, from 8 to 10 years old, running in and out of the burning stoves until the sweat literally pours down their bodies and the poor things become emaciated and enfeebled for life.[8]

He also remarked on the detrimental effect of the lack of ventilation in the finishing rooms.

A twelve-hour day was the norm, usually starting at 6.30 a.m. and perhaps finishing at 2 p.m. or 4 p.m. on Saturdays; however, hours might increase to enable large orders to be fulfilled. Working conditions were poor, particularly for those employed in the smaller potbanks. Apart from the long hours, the hot and dusty atmosphere and the exposure to toxic chemicals, the toilets might be in full view of the workforce. Dippers, who were responsible for glazing biscuit-fired ware before the second firing, were immersing their hands in lead oxide many times a day. Lead was absorbed through the skin and the workers would also be inhaling powdered lead dust. The dust could remain on the worker's clothing and thus be transferred to their home. One of the health hazards that resulted for women was an increased chance of miscarriage.

The Huddersfield Chronicle of 18 August 1886 reported on the case of 17-year-old Marian Ogden, a worker at the Burmantofts Pottery, Leeds who was claiming £1,500 damages as a result of going blind due to inhaling dust in the course of her work. The factory tried to lay the blame on Marian, claiming that there were printed rules stating the importance of hand washing and that they also provided a 'special acidulated drink', to nullify the effects of lead sulphate.

The ruling went in Marian's favour but the compensation that she was awarded was just £100.⁹

On 22 September 1898, the *Northern Daily Telegraph* reported as follows:

> The North Staffordshire Chamber of Commerce, which is mainly comprised of pottery manufacturers, was yesterday invited by the Potteries, Trades and Labour Council to co-operate to raise funds to assist a large number of pottery workers who, it was stated, are suffering from the effects of lead poisoning. The Chamber discussed the subject and Mr T. Arrowsmith moved a resolution which, while expressing sympathy with the sufferers, stated that the rules and precedent forbade them from helping. Mr E. Brain said the Chamber ought to pass a resolution condemning the exaggerated reports which had done the manufacturers much harm. Mr Arrowsmith's resolution was carried.¹⁰

Majolica ware became very popular in the late nineteenth century. The brightly coloured glazes that were required contained a higher lead content than other glazes. The 1880s saw the beginning of an awareness of the dangers of working with lead, particularly for dippers, majolica paintresses and glost placers. Many glost placers were male but females also took on this role. They worked in the ovens department, filling the saggers, or protective boxes, with dipped items before they were fired. They had to separate out individual pieces with different shaped spacers, known as thimbles, or stiles, to stop the ware from sticking together. From 1896, doctors and manufacturers had to report cases of lead poisoning contracted in factories and workshops. Forty per cent of those reported were pottery workers, significantly more than any other trade. Lead poisoning could result in blindness, fitting and paralysis.

Following a public enquiry, in 1898, the use of the most dangerous form of lead was banned, with no more than 5 per cent of the standard solution of lead allowable in the glazes; however, this was not easy to enforce. It was recommended that workers should be provided with protective clothing and there were age restrictions for those employed in the most dangerous roles, such as, dippers, majolica painters, glost placers and those involved in transfer making, colour dusting and china scouring. In 1898, the minimum age was 14 and this was raised to 15 the following year. From 1899, there were also regulations regarding the daily cleaning of the workshops.

For those living in the area around Stoke-on-Trent, working in the potbanks was the norm. Although the trade provided plenty of job opportunities for women, it was frequently at the cost of their health.

Mary Pankhurst's Story

With thanks to Ann Simcock for bringing Mary's story to my attention.

Mary's story is an interesting one. If her entries in the censuses are examined, there is no indication of her connection to the potbanks, nor, apart from the presence of an illegitimate child, is there any hint of her troubled family life. Mary was born about 1833 in Hanley, Staffordshire, the eldest of the six children of William Horatio and Edna Pankhurst. William's nephew was to become the husband of Emmeline Pankhurst, the notable campaigner for women's suffrage.

In the 1841 census, Mary can be found living with her mother and four younger sisters in Shelton, a suburb of Hanley, Staffordshire; her father was in London. We cannot tell if he had abandoned the family temporarily, or was away working. Like many young women, Mary went into service and at the age of 16, was employed by William Smith, a 'gentleman', in Withington in Lancashire. Back in Staffordshire with the family, her father was part of the pottery industry, working as a colour manufacturer. The following year, William, who went by his middle name of Horatio, was sentenced to fourteen years' transportation and was sent, via prisons in Stafford and Leeds, to Portsmouth Prison. While there, his deteriorating health meant that he was transferred to Dartmoor Prison, rather than being sent overseas and he died of tuberculosis at Dartmoor in 1854.

William Horatio's crime was one that involved other members of the family and was rooted in the industry in which he worked. He was convicted of receiving stolen goods and stealing borax from Charles Meigh and Sons' pottery. His wife, Edna, and eldest son, Henry, were also accused, along with William Pennington. Borax was an important and valuable ingredient used in the production of glazes for the pottery industry; there was also a local monopoly on its supply. William Horatio seized the opportunity to provide an alternative source of borax for pottery manufacturers and chemists. He recruited Pennington, who worked for Meigh and had access to the borax, while Henry acted as the go-between.

It was Henry Pankhurst, then aged 16, who was caught red-handed with a large quantity of borax and he admitted that, at the instigation of his father, he was collecting the stolen borax. Pennington confessed that he had been stealing borax from his employer for the past two years and that William Horatio had disposed of the stolen goods. Henry Pankhurst also implicated his mother, saying she knew of his intentions and had sewn the bags that were to contain the borax. In his evidence, William Pennington stated that he sold stolen borax to Pankhurst, his wife, boy or girl. Could this girl have been Mary? Her next eldest sister was only 11 at the time, so it seems likely.

Edna was discharged as she was considered to have been acting under coercion from her husband. Equally, young Henry was given a light sentence, on account of his youth and perceived pressure from his father and was to spend time in a reformatory.

With this family background, it is hardly surprising that Mary took solace elsewhere and by 1858, she was pregnant. In the October of that year, she planned to marry Joseph Caton, who was presumably the unborn child's father. The marriage register of St Luke's, Wellington, Hanley, Staffordshire contains just the couple's names and the date, with a note that was added the following year, which reads 'the parties did not attend according to arrangement, whereupon action for breach of promise of marriage and damages recovered'. Mary's daughter, Harriet, was born three months later.

It is Mary's relationship with Joseph, and consequent newspaper reports, that reveal that she worked in the pottery industry. In 1859, Mary appeared in court, having accused Joseph Caton of breach of promise. It seems that Mary was back in Staffordshire about the time of her father's conviction and was working as a gold grinder for G.F. Bowden's china manufactory in Tunstall. She was not living at home but lodging in Hanley with a Mrs Walsh. In court, Mr Bowden stated that Mary's work was entirely satisfactory and that she had always conducted herself with great propriety.

Gold decoration was popular on more expensive pieces of china; plates might be rimmed with gold, or gold might form part of the painted design. Gold grinding was responsible work, as the ingredients were valuable and Mary would have been working in a colour department, as her father had done. Mary's work involved grinding various ingredients on a slab in order to produce the oily substance that was painted onto the china. Gold powder would be mixed with oils and other ingredients, in a recipe that would be known only to those who were working with the gold.

Joseph's background might be regarded as less respectable. A former butcher, at the time of his involvement with Mary, he was helping his mother to run a gin palace in Burslem, following the death of his father. Weeks before the intended marriage, Joseph had moved Mary to live with a Mrs Wrench and he gave Mrs Wrench money to have the banns called. It may be that the plan was to save money by both residing in the same parish, so that only one set of banns would be required. On the appointed day, Mary arrived at the church but Joseph did not appear. Mrs Wrench sought him out and begged him to attend but he abandoned Mary.

Once Harriet was born, Mary's friends helped her to serve Joseph with a maintenance order and he was paying 2s 6d a week for Harriet's keep. Perhaps that was sufficient for childcare, so that Mary could continue working, or maybe mother and child were forced to live on 2s 6d a week. Understandably not content with this financial arrangement, Mary brought the 1859 court case, claiming for damages for breach of promise. In court, it was stated that, on the death of his mother, Joseph was due to inherit £500 from his father's estate; perhaps Mary was aware of this. Mary was granted £50.

Did Joseph feel that, having paid this sum, he was somehow entitled to sexual favours from Mary? Was Mary attracted by Joseph's irresistible charm? Or did the couple just drift back together despite the rift? In 1861, Mary was living in Hope Street, Shelton, with 2-year-old Harriet. No occupation was listed for Mary and she no longer appears to be with Mrs Wrench. Mary was, however, once again pregnant. Joseph meanwhile was still with his mother at the Black Lion Inn in Burslem. Their son, Thomas Joseph Caton Pankhurst, to be known as Joseph Caton, was born a few months later.

When Mary became pregnant for the third time, in 1862, Joseph and Mary finally married. A look at the 1871 census suggests that they were in a stable relationship, living at 12 Sidney Street, Shelton in Hanley, with Joseph returning to butcher's work. Children had continued to arrive regularly every two years with the youngest, William, having been born in the second quarter of 1867. Wilmot, who was born in 1869, had died in infancy. At the time of the 1871 census, Mary was pregnant with what was to be the seventh of their eight children. Despite the evenly spaced offspring, there had been an hiatus in the relationship.

With Mary pregnant once again, in July 1865, Joseph Caton, a beerseller of Lyndhurst Street, was declared bankrupt. In the April of 1865, Joseph, perhaps realising his financial position, had deserted his pregnant wife and three children and left for Australia. Following the bankruptcy proceedings of July 1865, the *Staffordshire Advertiser* of 29 September 1866 contained a notice for the auction of the household furniture, public house fixtures and brewing plant belonging to Mr Joseph Caton.[11] It seems that Joseph's inheritance was gone and the family was homeless. The Married Women's Property Act was not passed until 1882, legally all Mary's possessions, with the exception of the clothes she stood up in belonged to Joseph.

In June 1866, the *Sussex Advertiser* reported that a Mary Pankhurst had taken out a protection order against her husband, a butcher.[12] She was using the 1857 Matrimonial Causes Act, which meant that a husband who deserted his wife had no right to her earnings. By the terms of the act, a divorced or legally separated woman had the same property rights as a single woman. Is this Mary Caton reverting to her maiden name? There is no record of Joseph Caton's trip to Australia but this is before the commencement of complete passenger lists. If this is the same couple, did Joseph actually go abroad, or was it a ploy to preserve Mary's earnings? This incident hasn't been found in the press elsewhere, so the Sussex location is unexpected. There are Pankhurst families in Sussex, although no other Mary with a butcher as a husband has been found.

In 1881, Joseph and Mary were back living together at 29 Hampton Street, Shelton, with their five youngest surviving children. Their 17-year-old daughter, Lavinia, was a potter's paintress. In the October of 1881, Mary's brother, Francis Pankhurst, who already had a criminal record for larceny, was accused of assaulting Joseph

Caton, who was said to be living in the same house. Following an altercation, which also involved Joseph's sister, a Mrs Milliner, Francis struck Joseph on the head with a poker. Francis was found guilty but because he was judged to have been provoked, was fined just £1.

The family cannot be found in 1891 but by 1901, Mary, describing herself as a widow, was living with her married daughter Henrietta. Joseph, however, was very much alive and living with another married daughter, Lavinia Brown, claiming to be married. This did not represent a rift among the children, as after Mary died, in 1903, Joseph can be found living with Henrietta in 1911; he died in 1914.

Mary's story and the area in which she lived her life, is inextricable from the pottery trade. The majority of her family, friends and neighbours, as well as Mary herself, worked in the pottery industry; pollution from the potbanks would have pervaded her home. Although the details of their relationship remain elusive, Mary's tenacity in taking Joseph to court makes her stand out from many women of her time.

References

Chapter 1

1. Few, Janet *Remember Then: Women's Memories Of 1946–1969 and How to Write Your Own* Family History Partnership (2015) p.48.
2. For more information about the history and role of the common, see **www.acraew.org.uk/history-common-land-and-village-greens** and **www.nationalarchives.gov.uk/help-with-your-research/research-guides/common-lands/**.
3. A history of knitting can be found at **www.knitty.com/ISSUEspring06/FEAThistory101.html**.
4. A history of the sewing machine can be found at **www.moah.org/stitches/index.html**.
5. For background on *The English Woman's Domestic Magazine* see **www.bl.uk/collection-items/the-englishwomans-domestic-magazine** and for online copies see **http://onlinebooks.library.upenn.edu/webbin/serial?id=englishwomansdomestic**.
6. Few, Janet *Remember Then: Women's Memories of 1946–1969*, p.193.

Chapter 2

1. *The Daily Mirror* 21 November 1918 p.5 cols. b & c.

Chapter 3

1. Beeton, Isabella *Mrs Beeton's Book of Household Management* S.O. Beeton (1861) p.21.
2. Ibid. p.980.
3. Woolley, Hannah *The Compleat Servant-maid: or, the young maiden's and family's daily companion* first published in 1677, Gale ECCO Print (9th edition 1719) p.15.

4. Beeton, Isabella *Mrs Beeton's Book of Household Management*, p.1001.
5. Ibid. p.1005.
6. British Weekly Commissioners *Toilers in London; or, inquiries concerning female labour in the metropolis* Hodder and Stoughton (1889) p.79.

Chapter 4

1. Grof, Lazlo L. *Children of Straw* Baron (2002) p.50.
2. Few, Martha unpublished, untitled essay for The Open University course A173 (2008).
3. Grof, Lazlo L. *Children of Straw*, p.65.

Chapter 5

1. Bryant and May's company records are held at Hackney Archives in London.

Chapter 6

1. British Weekly Commissioners *Toilers in London; or, inquiries concerning female labour in the metropolis* Hodder and Stoughton (1889) pp.66–7.

Chapter 7

1. Mayhew, Henry *London Labour and the London Poor* Griffin, Bohn and Co. (1862) p.216.
2. Ibid. p.213.
3. Chrisman-Campbell, Kimberly 'The Face of Fashion: milliners in eighteenth-century visual culture' in *Journal for eighteenth-century studies* (Vol. 25:2 2002) pp.157–71.
4. Campbell, R. *The London Tradesman* T. Gardner (1747) p.207.
5. Horne, Charles *Serious Thoughts on the Miseries of Seduction and Prostitution: with a full account of the evils that produce them* (1783) p.51.
6. *The Kentish Gazette* 26 June 1789 p.2 col. c.
7. *The Norfolk Chronicle* 7 January 1786 p.4 col. a.

Chapter 8

1. Although unicorn horn sounds like an ingredient that would prove impossible to acquire, unicorn horn may also refer to the plant *Proboscidea? louisianica*, although this was not brought to England until 1731. Narwal tusks were sometimes passed off as unicorn horns.
2. A manuscript in private hands.
3. Few, Janet *Remember Then: Women's Memories of 1946–1969*, pp.139–41.

Chapter 9

1. Letter from Florence Nightingale to Sir Thomas Watson 19 January 1867, quoted in Gaffney, R. 'Women as Doctors and Nurses' in Checkland, O.; Lamb, M. *Health Care as Social History* Cambridge University Press (1982) pp.134–48.
2. See also Chapter 21 for more about the role of the wet nurse.

Chapter 10

1. Few, Janet *Remember Then: Women's Memories of 1946–1969*, pp.90–91.
2. Best, Michael (ed.) *The English Housewife – Gervase Markham* McGill-Queen's University Press (1986) first published in 1615 p.89.
3. Kettilby, Mary et al. *A Collection of above Three Hundred Receipts in Cookery* Richard Wilkin (1714) Nabu Press (2010) p.114.

Chapter 12

1. Best, Michael R. (ed.) *The English Housewife – Gervase Markham* p.170.
2. Woolley, Hannah *The Compleat Servant-maid*, p.17.
3. Best, Michael (ed.) *The English Housewife – Gervase Markham*, pp.176–8.
4. Hazlitt, William Carew *Old Cookery Books and Ancient Cuisine* Elliot Stock (1886) p.125.

Chapter 13

1. www.statista.com/statistics/878429/average-time-spent-cleaning-one-s-home-by-region-united-kingdom-uk accessed 14 November 2023.
2. *The English Woman's Domestic Magazine* Clarke, Beeton and Co. Volume 3 (1854) p.390.
3. Beeton, Isabella *Mrs Beeton's Book of Household Management*, p.988.
4. Few, Janet *Remember Then: Women's Memories of 1946–1969*, p.38.
5. Ibid. p.39.
6. Ibid. p.40.

Chapter 14

1. Palliser, Mrs Bury, Jourdain, Margaret and Dryden, Alice *A History of Lace* Sampson, Low, Son and Marston (1865) p.281.
2. Act 2, scene iv (1601).
3. www.bbc.co.uk/devon/content/articles/2007/08/07/honiton_lace_lessons_feature.shtml accessed 22 November 2023.
4. The 6th Report of the Medical Officer of the Children's Employment Commission 1864.

Chapter 15

1. Meigs, Charles D. *Obstetrics: the science and the art* Henry C. Lea (5th edition 1867) p.373.
2. Meigs, Charles D. *On the Nature, Signs and Treatment of Childbed Fevers* Blanchard and Lea (1854) p.104.
3. CAMPOP: Populations past www.populationspast.org. Geoff's Genealogy: Life and Death in the Nineteenth Century www.geoffsgenealogy.co.uk/other-articles/life-death-in-the-19th-century both accessed 27 January 2022.
4. Woolley, Hannah *The Compleat Servant-maid*, p.8.
5. A blouse.
6. Spaeth, Louis A. *Coming Motherhood* (1907). Although this book was published in 1907, the original edition was produced in 1863 and it is unknown how much the text had been updated,

References 153

if at all. Quoted on **https://theweek.com/articles/454290/how-give-birth-100-years-ago** accessed 23 February 2024.
7. Lysol was a caustic disinfectant. The equivalent of Dettol.
8. Fry, Henry Davidson, *Maternity* Neale (1907) quoted on **https://theweek.com/articles/454290/how-give-birth-100-years-ago** accessed 23 February 2024.
9. Spaeth, Louis A. *Coming Motherhood* (1907).

Chapter 16

1. *The Manchester Courier* 22 January 1877 p.3 col. e.

Chapter 18

1. Few, Janet *Remember Then: Women's Memories of 1946–1969*, pp.42–3.
2. Few, Janet *Housework Memories* **https://janetfew.wixsite.com/grannystales/memories** accessed 8 July 2023.
3. Few, Janet *Remember Then: Women's Memories of 1946–1969*, p.45.
4. Ibid. p.42.

Chapter 19

1. Thackrah, C. Turner *The Effects of the Principal Arts, Trades and Professions and of Civic States and Habits of Living on Health and Longevity: with particular reference to the trades and manufacturers of Leeds and suggestions for removal of many of the agents, which produce disease and shorten the duration of life* Longman, Orme, Brown & Green (1831) p.20.
2. Ibid. pp.42–3.
3. *The Morning Chronicle* 3 December 1849 p.5 col. e.
4. Mayhew, Henry *London Labour and the London Poor* Volume 2 Griffin, Bohn and Co. (1861) p.30.
5. *Derby Daily Telegraph* 29 October 1903 p.3 col. g.

Chapter 22

1. Few, Janet *Remember Then: Women's Memories of 1946–1969* p.132.

2. Mulcaster, Richard *Positions: wherein those primitive circumstances be examined, which are necessarie for the training of children, either for skill in their booke, or health in their bodie* Thomas Vautollier (1561) p.167.
3. Macaulay, Thomas Babbington *Speeches of Lord Macaulay*, corrected by himself Issue 52 Longman, Green, Longman and Roberts (1860) p.479.
4. *The Brecon County Times* 26 November 1925 p.2 cols. a & b.

Chapter 23

1. McFarland, Joan 'Pottery Industry: a case of lost potential' in *Atlantis* Vol. 11.1 (autumn 1985) p.36.
2. Her Majesties Commissioners on the Employment of Children and Young Persons in the District of the Staffordshire Potteries and on the Actual State, Condition and Treatment of such Children and Young Persons HMSO (1841). The full text is available at **www.thepotteries.org/history/scriven.htm**.
3. First Report to the Children's Employment Commission HMSO (1863).
4. Her Majesties Commissioners on the Employment of Children and Young Persons in the District of the Staffordshire Potteries and on the Actual State, Condition and Treatment of such Children and Young Persons HMSO (1841). The full text is available at **www.thepotteries.org/history/scriven.htm**.
5. Ibid.
6. Ibid.
7. Ibid.
8. First Report to the Children's Employment Commission HMSO (1863).
9. *The Huddersfield Chronicle* 18 August 1886 p.4 col. c.
10. *Northern Daily Telegraph* 22 September 1898 p.2 col. f.
11. *Staffordshire Advertiser* 29 September 1866 p.8 col. c.
12. *Sussex Advertiser* 30 June 1866 p.3 col. a.

Selected Further Reading

General

Baudino, Isabelle; Carré, Jacques and Révauger, Cecile (eds.) *The Invisible Woman: Aspects of Women's Work in Eighteenth-Century Britain* Ashgate (2005)

Bradley, R.M. *The English Housewife in the Seventeenth and Eighteenth Centuries* Edward Arnold (1912)

British Weekly Commissioners *Toilers in London; or, inquiries concerning female labour in the metropolis* Hodder and Stoughton (1889)

Chrystal, Paul *Women at Work in World Wars I and II: Factories, Farms and The Military and Civil Services* Pen and Sword (2024)

Clark, Alice *Working Life of Women in the Seventeenth Century* Routledge, London and New York (1982)

Davidson, Caroline *A Woman's Work is Never Done* Chatto & Windus (1982)

Emm, Adele *Tracing Your Female Ancestors: A Guide for Family Historians* Pen and Sword (2019)

Few, Janet *Coffers, Clysters, Comfrey and Coifs: The Lives of Our Seventeenth-Century Ancestors* Family History Partnership (2012)

Few, Janet *Remember Then: Women's Memories Of 1946–1969 and How to Write Your Own* Family History Partnership (2015)

Flanders, Judith Prostitution https://victorianeradotblog.wordpress.com/2018/11/09/prostitution-in-the-19th-century/

Fraser, Antonia *The Weaker Vessel: Women's Lot in the Seventeenth Century* Vintage Books (1984)

Gowing, Laura *Ingenious Trade: Women and Work in Seventeenth-Century London* Cambridge University Press (2021)

Hill, Bridget *Women Alone: Spinsters in England 1650–1850* Yale University Press (2001)

Hill, Bridget *Women, Work and Sexual Politics in Eighteenth-Century England* Routledge (2005)

Hole, Christina *The English Housewife in the Seventeenth Century* Chatto & Windus (1953)

Joyce, Fraser *Prostitution and the Nineteenth Century: in search of the 'Great Social Evil'*. https://warwick.ac.uk/fac/cross_fac/iatl/research/reinvention/archive/volume1issue1/joyce/

Karsland, Veva (aka Stephens, Amy) *Women and their Work* Sampson, Low, Marston and Co. (1891)

Knight, Lynn *The Button Box: The Story of Women in The Twentieth Century Told Through the Clothes That They Wore* Vintage (2017)

Lawrence, Anne *Women in England 1500–1760: A Social History* W & N (2005)

Leyser, Henrietta *Medieval Women: A Social History of Women in England 450–1500* W & N (2005)

Lyttelton, The Hon. Mrs Arthur *Women and their Work* Methuen (1901) https://babel.hathitrust.org/cgi/pt?id=mdp.39015064805909&view=1up&seq=9.

Mitchell, Sally *The New Girl: Girls' Culture in England 1880–1915* Columbia University Press (1995)

Newby, Jennifer *Women's Lives 1800–1939: Researching Women's Social History 1800–1939* Pen and Sword (2011)

Pennington, S. and Westover, B. *A Hidden Workforce: Homeworkers in England 1850–1985* Macmillan Education (1989)

Perkin, Joan *Victorian Women* John Murray (1994)

Pinchbeck, Ivy *Women Workers and the Industrial Revolution 1750–1850* Virago (1981)

Rendall, Jane *Women in an Industrialising Society: England 1759–1880* Blackwell (1991)

Roberts, Elizabeth *A Woman's Place: An Oral History of Working-Class Women 1890–1940* Blackwell (1984)

Read, Sara *Maids, Wives, Widows; Exploring Early Modern Women's Lives 1540–1740* Pen and Sword (2015)

Simonton, Deborah *A History Of European Women's Work, 1700 to the Present* Routledge (1998)

Steinbach, Susie *Women in England 1760–1914; A Social History* Phoenix (2005)

Taylor, Mrs *Practical Hints to Young Females on the Duties of a Wife, a Mother, and a Mistress of the Family* Taylor & Hessey (1815)

Tolan, Elspeth *Hidden in Plain Sight: Finding Working-Class Women in The National Archives* (2022) https://blog.nationalarchives.gov.uk/finding-working-class-women-in-the-national-archives/

Turner, Mary *The Women's Century: A Celebration of Changing Roles* TNA (2006)

Ward, Margaret *The Female Line: Researching Your Female Ancestors* Countryside Books (2003)

Ward, Margaret *Female Occupations: Women's Employment from 1840–1950* Countryside Books (2008)

West, Jane *Letters to a Young Lady in which the Duties and Character of Women are Considered* O. Penniman & Co. (1806)

Woolley, Hannah *The Compleat Servant-maid: or, the young maiden's and family's daily companion* Gale ECCO Print (9th edition 1719)

Forgotten Women https://afewforgottenwomen.wixsite.com/affw. This site includes resources for women's history.

Chapter 1

Adlington, Lucy *Stitches in Time: The Story of The Clothes We Wear* Random House Books (2016)

Grafton, Carol Belanger *Victorian Fashions: A Pictorial Archive with Over 1000 Illustrations of Women's Fashions from 1855–1903* Dover Publications (2012)

Richmond, Vivienne *Clothing the Poor in Nineteenth-Century England* Cambridge University Press (2016)

Shrimpton, Jayne *British Working Dress: Occupational Clothing 1750–1950* Shire Publications (2012)

Styles, John *The Dress of the People: Everyday Fashion in Eighteenth-Century England* Yale University Press (2008)

Waugh, Norah *The Cut of Men's Clothes 1600–1930* Routledge (1987)

Waugh, Norah *The Cut of Women's Clothes 1600–1930* Faber & Faber (1994)

A Fashion Era www.fashion-era.com/index.htm a gateway site

Victorian Clothing www.vam.ac.uk/content/articles/h/history-of-fashion-1840-1900/

Twentieth-Century Clothing www.thepeoplehistory.com/fashions.html

Children's Clothing http://fashion-history.lovetoknow.com/fashion-history-eras/history-childrens-clothing this site includes ideas for further reading and additional links.

Women's Clothing http://mymodernmet.com/womens-fashion-history/

Chapter 2

Harding, Phil *The British Shell Shortage of the First World War* Fonthill Media (2015)

Hymas, Jackie *Bomb Girls: Britain's Secret Army: The Munitions Women of World War II* John Blake (2014)
Williams, M.A. *A Forgotten Army: The Female Munitions Workers of South Wales, 1939–1945* University of Wales Press (2002)
Woollacott, Angela *On Her Their Lives Depend: Munitions Workers in The Great War* University of California Press (1994)

The Munitionettes, National Records of Scotland www.nrscotland.gov.uk/research/learning/first-world-war/the-munitionettes-and-the-work-of-women-in-the-first-world-war
Historic England First World War Munitions Factories https://historicengland.org.uk/research/current/discover-and-understand/military/first-world-war-home-front/land/munitions-factories/
Imperial War Museum's *A Day in the Life of a Munitions Worker* a series of video clips by Gemma Lawrence www.iwm.org.uk/history/a-day-in-the-life-of-a-munitions-worker
Imperial War Museum's *The Dangers of Working in a Munitions Factory* www.iwm.org.uk/history/9-women-reveal-the-dangers-of-working-in-a-first-world-war-munitions-factory
The Barnbow Factory https://historicengland.org.uk/whats-new/news/fww-munitions-factory-given-heritage-protection

Chapter 3

Beeton, Mrs Isabella *Mrs Book of Household Management* London (1861)
Horn, Pamela *Life Below Stairs in the Twentieth Century* Sutton Publishing (2001)
Horn, Pamela *The Rise and Fall of the Victorian Servant* Sutton Publishing (1995)
Mansell, Charmian *Female Servants in Early Modern England* Oxford University Press (2024)
May, Trevor *The Victorian Domestic Servant* Shire Publications (2006)
Woolley, Hannah *The Compleat Servant-maid: or the young maiden's and family's daily companion* 9th edition London (1719 – available in facsimile form)

Women and domestic service in Victorian Society www.thehistorypress.co.uk/articles/women-and-domestic-service-in-victorian-society/

Chapter 4

Clarke, E. 'Plait and Plaiters' in *Cassell's Family Magazine* (c.1882)
Davis, Jean *Straw Plait* Shire Publications Ltd. (1981)

Goose, Nigel *How Saucy did it Make the Poor? The Straw Plait and Hat Trades, Illegitimate Fertility and the Family in Nineteenth-Century Hertfordshire* https://uhra.herts.ac.uk/bitstream/handle/2299/391/103472.pdf?sequence=1

Goose, Nigel 'The Straw Plait and Hat Trades' in Short, D. (ed.) *An Atlas of Hertfordshire History* University of Hertfordshire Press (2006)

Grof, Lazlo L. *Children of Straw* Baron (2002)

Horn, Pamela *The Buckinghamshire Straw Plait Trade in Victorian England* www.bucksas.org.uk/rob/rob_19_1_42.pdf

Horn, Pamela *Labouring Life in the Victorian Countryside* Sutton Publishing (1987)

Main Veronica *Straw Plaiting: Heritage Techniques for Hats, Trimmings, Bags and Baskets* Bloomsbury Publishing (2023)

Pennington, S. and Westover, B. *A Hidden Workforce, Homeworkers in England 1850–1985* Macmillan Education (1989)

Staniforth, Arthur *Straw and Strawcraftsmen* Shire Publications Ltd. (1991)

The History of Straw Plait in Hertfordshire www.hertfordshire-genealogy.co.uk/data/occupations/straw-plait.htm; www.prestonherts.co.uk/page222.html

Straw Plaiting Tools https://thestrawshop.com/splitters

Straw Plaiters www.geni.com/projects/Straw-Plaiters/30411

Chapter 5

Beaver, Patrick *The Match Makers: The Story of Bryant & May* Henry Melland (1985)

Beer, Reg *Matchgirls Strike 1888: The Struggle Against Sweated Labour in London's East End* by National Museum of Labour History (1979)

Charlton, John *It Just Went Like Tinder; The Mass Movement and New Unionism in Britain 1889: A Socialist History* Redwoods (1999)

Emsley, John *The Shocking History of Phosphorus: A Biography of the Devil's Element* Macmillan (2000)

Stafford, Ann *A Match to Fire the Thames* Hodder and Stoughton (1961)

Threlfall, Richard E. *The Story of 100 years of Phosphorus Making 1851–1951* Albright & Wilson (1951)

Legacies UK Local History to You
www.bbc.co.uk/legacies/work/england/london/article_1.shtml
British Library www.bl.uk/learning/timeline/item106451.html

Chapter 6

Frank, Peter *Yorkshire Fisherfolk* Phillimore (2002)

Herring Girls www.nefa.net/nefajnr/archive/peopleandlife/sea/fisherfolk2.htm

The Ferrow Fishwives www.johngraycentre.org/people/east-lothian-folk/the-fisherrow-fishwives/

Nineteenth-century Salt Fish Markets 1850–1914 www.heritage.nf.ca/articles/economy/salt-fish-markets-1850.php

Chapter 7

Bartley, Paula *Prostitution: Prevention and Reform in England 1860–1914* Routledge (2004)

Broglin, C.G. Jana Sloan *Hookers, Crooks and Kooks: Part 1 Hookers* Heritage Books (2007)

Finnegan, Frances *Poverty and Prostitution: A Study of Victorian Prostitutes in York* Cambridge University Press (1979)

Hartley, Jenny *Charles Dickens and the House of the Fallen Women* Methuen (2009)

Hemyng, B. 'Prostitution in London', in Mayhew, H. *London Labour and the London Poor: Volume IV Those Who Will Not Work; Comprising Prostitutes, Thieves, Swindlers and Beggars* Dover Publications (1862)

Mahood, L. *The Magdalenes: Prostitution in The Nineteenth Century* Routledge (1990)

McHugh, Paul *Prostitution and Victorian Social Reform: The Campaign Against the Contagious Diseases Act* Routledge (2004)

Walkowitz, Judith R. *Prostitution and Victorian Society: Women, Class and State* Cambridge University Press (1982)

Flanders, Judith *Prostitution* www.bl.uk/romantics-and-victorians/articles/prostitution

Joyce, Fraser *Prostitution and the Nineteenth Century: In Search of the 'Great Social Evil'*

https://warwick.ac.uk/fac/cross_fac/iatl/reinvention/archive/volume1issue1/joyce

Records of prostitution at TNA https://discovery.nationalarchives.gov.uk/details/r/b4de3e9e-cf9b-477a-9935-c33b22a49a20

Revisiting Dickens: prostitution in Victorian England https://revisitingdickens.wordpress.com/prostitution-victorian/

Cyndi's List www.cyndislist.com/occupations/prostitutes/

Chapter 8

Beeton, Isabella *Mrs Beeton's Book of Household Management*
Best, Michael R. (ed.) Markham, Gervase *The English Housewife* McGill-Queens University Press (1986) first published in 1615
Culpeper, Nicholas *Culpeper's Complete Herbal* Wordsworth Editions Limited (2007) first published in 1652
Downloadable edition of Culpeper's Complete Herbal **https://archive.org/details/culpeperscomplet00culpuoft**
Extracts from John French's Art of Distillation 1653 **www.levity.com/alchemy/jfren_1.html**
Gerard, John *Gerard's Herbal* Studio Editions Limited (1994) first published in 1633
Kettilby, Mary et. al. *A Collection of Above Three Hundred Receipts in Cookery*
Minter, Sue *The Apothecaries' Garden: A History of Chelsea Physic Garden* Sutton Publishing Limited (2003)
Stobart, Anne *Household Medicine in Seventeenth-Century England* Bloomsbury Academic (2016)
Wesley, John *Primitive Physic: An Easy and Natural Method of Curing Most Diseases* Leopold Classic Library (2017) first published in 1761
Woolley, Hannah *The Compleat Servant-maid*

Chapter 9

Abel-Smith, Brian *A History of the Nursing Profession* Heinemann (1960)
Achterberg, J. *Woman as Healer: A Comprehensive Survey from Prehistoric Times to the Present Day* Rider (2013)
Baly, Monica E. *A History of the Queen's Nursing Institute* Groom Helm (1987)
Bourdillon, H. *Women as Healers: A History of Women and Medicine* Cambridge University Press (1988)
Cowen, Ruth *A Nurse at the Front: The Great War Diaries of Sister Edith Appleton* Simon & Schuster (2012)
English, D. *Witches, Midwives, and Nurses: A History of Female Healers* The Feminist Press (1973)
Hay, Ian *One Hundred Years of Army Nursing* Cassell (1953)
Helmstadter, C. & Godden, J. *Nursing before Nightingale 1815–1899* Ashgate Publishing (2011)
Higgs, Michelle *Life in the Victorian Hospital* The History Press (2009)
Higgs, Michelle *Tracing your Medical Ancestors: A Guide for Family Historians* Pen and Sword (2011)

Pavey, Agnes *The Story of the Growth of Nursing* revised ed. Faber & Faber (1959)
Piggott, Juliet *Queen Alexandra's Royal Army Nursing Corps* Pen and Sword (1990)
Stocks, Mary *A Hundred Years of District Nursing* George Allen & Unwin (1960)
Summers, Anne *Angels and Citizens: British Women as Military Nurses 1854–1914* Threshold Press Ltd. (2000)
Tyrer, Nicola *Sister in Arms: British Army Nurses Tell Their Story* Phoenix (2009)

History of Nursing www.nursingschoolhub.com/history-nursing/
A Brief History of Nursing in the UK http://memoriesofnursing.uk/articles/a-brief-history-of-nursing-in-the-uk
Robson-Mainwaring, Laura *Ethel Gordon Fenwick: The Story of The First State Registered Nurse* TNA blog post (2021) https://blog.nationalarchives.gov.uk/ethel-gordon-fenwick-the-story-of-the-first-state-registered-nurse

Chapter 10

Beeton, Mrs Isabella *Mrs Beeton's Book of Household* Management (1861)
Best, Michael R. (ed.)*The English Housewife – Gervase Markham*
Black, Maggie *The Medieval Cook Book* British Museum Press (2012)
Black, Maggie *Victorian Cookery* English Heritage (2004)
Brears, Peter *Food and Cooking in Seventeenth-Century Britain* English Heritage (1985)
Brears, Peter *Stuart Cookery* English Heritage (2004)
Brears, Peter *Tudor Cookery* English Heritage (2004)
Dawson, Thomas *The Good Housewife's Jewel* Southover Press (1996) first published in 1596/7
Digby, Sir Kenelm *The Closet of Sir Kenelm Digby Opened* Echo Library (2007) first published in 1669
Evelyn, John *Acetaria: A Discourse of Sallets* Prospect Books (1996) first published in 1699
French, Richard Valpy *Nineteen Centuries of Drink in England: A History* Longmans Green (1884)
Glasse, Hannah *The Art of Cookery Made Plain and Easy* 2015 Dover (2015) first published in 1747
Hartley, Dorothy *Food in England* Piatkus (1954)
Hazlitt, William Carew *Old Cookery Books and Ancient Cuisine* Elliot Stock (1886)
Henderson, William Augustus *The Housekeeper's Instructor* J.C. Schnebbeli (1806)

Kettilby, Mary et. al. *A Collection of above Three Hundred Receipts in Cookery*
M., W. *The Compleat Cook* Prospect Books (1984) first published in 1655
M., W. *A Queen's Delight* Prospect Books (1984) first published in 1671
Stead, Jennifer *Food and Cooking in Eighteenth-Century Britain* English Heritage (1985)
Tannahill, Reay *Food in History* Penguin (1988)
Woolley, Hannah *The Queen-like Closet or Rich Cabinet* The Essential Book Market (2007) first published in 1672

Food Calendar and Timeline www.foodreference.com/html/html/yearonlytimeline.html
Food Timeline www.foodtimeline.org
Gode Cookery C17th English Recipes www.godecookery.com/engrec/engrec.html
The Recipes Project http://recipes.hypotheses.org
The Regency Cook https://paulcouchman.co.uk/
Savoring the Past C18th and early C19th cook books https://savoringthepast.net/
A Timeline of Food www.localhistories.org/foodtime.html

Chapter 11

Leyland, N.L. & Troughton, J.E. *Glovemaking in West Oxfordshire: The Craft and its History* Oxford City and County Museum (1974)
Redwood, Mike *Gloves and Glovemaking* Shire Publications (2016)
Robbins, Denny *Gloving in Tintinhull* (2023) https://drive.google.com/file/d/10VS3hYt9SceSmGPOpGpmzOEvI5V_reSm/view

The History of Gloves and their Significance www.fashionintime.org/history-gloves-significance/

Chapter 12

Ingram, Arthur *Dairying Bygones* Shire Publications (2008)

Chapter 13

Davidson, Caroline *A Woman's Work is Never Done: A History of Housework in the British Isles 1650–1950* Chatto & Windus (1983)

Chapter 14

Bartlett, Liz *Lace Villages* Arima Publishing (2006)
Kraatz, Anne *Lace: History and Fashion* Rizzoli International Publications (1989)
Levey, Santina *Lace, A History* Maney (1990)
Nottingham, Pamela *The Technique of Bobbin Lace* Batsford (1976)
Wright, Thomas *The Romance of the Lace Pillow* Ruth Bean Publishers (1982)

The Lace Guild www.laceguild.org/craft/index.html
Debate on the connection between the Huguenots and lacemaking, with many useful links https://churchmousec.wordpress.com/2015/08/25/huguenots-and-englands-lace-making-industry/
Goldenberg, Samuel L. *Lace, its origin and history* Brentano's (1904) https://en.wikisource.org/wiki/Lace,_Its_Origin_and_History

Chapter 15

Cassidy, Tina *Birth: A History* Chatto & Windus (2007)
Cox, Jessica *Confinement: The Hidden History of Maternal Bodies in Nineteenth-Century Britain* The History Press (2023)
Fox, Sarah *Giving Birth in Eighteenth-Century England* University of London Press (2022)
Fox, Sarah and Brazier, Margaret 'The Regulation of Midwives in England c.1500–1902' in *Medical Law International* Vol. 20.4 (2020) https://journals.sagepub.com/doi/10.1177/0968533220976174
Gelis, Jacques *History of Childbirth, Fertility, Pregnancy and Birth in Early Modern Europe* Polity (1996)
Hobby, Elaine (ed.) Sharp, Jane *The Midwives' Book or, The Whole Art of Midwifery Discovered* Oxford University Press (1999) first published in 1671
Marland, Hilary *The Art of Midwifery: Early Modern Midwives in Europe* Routledge (1994)
Staras, Tania 'A Brief History of District Midwifery' in *AIMS Journal* Vol. 34 no. 3 (2022) www.aims.org.uk/journal/item/history-district-midwifery
Thomas, Ian (ed.) Culpeper, Nicholas *Book Of Birth; A Seventeenth-Century Guide to Having Lusty Children* Webb and Bower (1985) first published in 1651

Chapter 16

Bensley, Lin *The Village Shop* Shire Publications (2008)

Cox, Pamela and Hobley, Annabel *Shopgirls: The True Story of Life Behind the Counter* Hutchinson (2014)

Wild, Jonathan *Literature of the 1900s: The Great Edwardian Emporium* Edinburgh University Press (2017)

Winstanley, Michael *The Shopkeeper's World 1830–1914* Manchester University Press (1983)

Chapter 17

Adie, Kate *Corsets to Camouflage: Woman and War* Hodder & Stoughton (2003)

Antrobus, Stuart *'We Wouldn't Have Missed It for the World': The Women's Land Army in Bedfordshire, 1939–1950* Book Castle (2008)

Bates, Martha *Snagging Turnips and Scaling Muck: The Women's Land Army in Westmorland* Kendal Helm Press (2001)

Clarke, Gill *The Women's Land Army: A Portrait* Sansom and Co. Ltd. (2008)

De la Haye, Amy *Land Girls: Cinderellas of the Soil* Royal Pavilion Libraries & Museums (2009)

Gordon, Dee *Voices from History: Essex Land Girls* The History Press (2015)

Jolly, Emma *My Ancestor was a Woman at War* Society of Genealogists (2014)

Kramer, Ann *Land Girls and their Impact* Remember When (2008)

Mant, Joan *All Muck No Medals: Landgirls by Landgirls* Book Guild Publishing Ltd. (1994)

Rattray, Veronica *My Land Girl Years* Athena Press (2009)

Scott, Caroline *Holding the Home Front: The Women's Land Army in the First World War* Pen and Sword (2020)

Storey, Neil R. and Housego, Molly *The Women's Land Army* Shire Publications (2012)

Twinch, Carol *Women on the Land: Their Story During Two World Wars* Lutterworth Press (1990)

Tyrer, Nicola *They Fought in the Fields: The Women's Land Army: The Story of a Forgotten Victory* Mandarin (1997)

Women's Land Army and Timber Corps www.womenslandarmy.co.uk

National Archives Research Guide: The Women's Land Army www.nationalarchives.gov.uk/help-with-your-research/research-guides/womens-land-army

Chapter 18

Malcolmson, Patricia E. *English Laundresses: A Social History 1850–1930* University of Illinois Press (1986)
Sambrook, Pamela *Laundry Bygones* Shire Publications (2004)
Sewell, Brian *Smoothing Irons* Midas Books (1977)

Old and Interesting www.oldandinteresting.com/history-of-washing-clothes.aspx
This is the Way we Wash the Clothes in the eighteenth and early nineteenth centuries https://kimrendfeld.wordpress.com/2012/09/26/laundry-in-the-18th-and-early-19th-centuries/
Victorian Laundry www.vintageconnection.net/VictorianLaundry.htm

Chapter 19

Aspin, Chris *The Cotton Industry* Shire Publications (2003)
Aspin, Chris *The Woollen Industry* Shire Publications (2006)
Jubb, Samuel *The History of the Shoddy-trade: Its Rise, Progress, and Present Position* Houlston & Wright (1860)
Thackrah, C. Turner *The Effects of the Principal Arts, Trades and Professions and of Civic States and Habits of Living on Health and Longevity: with particular reference to the trades and manufacturers of Leeds and suggestions for removal of many of the agents, which produce disease and shorten the duration of life* Longman, Orme, Brown & Green (1831)

The Lancashire Cotton Industry www.cottontimes.co.uk
A Time-line of Textile Machinery www.thoughtco.com/textile-machinery-industrial-revolution-4076291

Chapter 20

Johns, Thelma *Dorset Buttons: Handstitched in Dorset for over 300 years* Natula Publications (2012)
McDowell, Anna *The Dorset Button Industry: A Modern-Day Instruction Manual* Independent Publishing Network (2017)
The Dorset Button Industry, Dorset Ancestors https://dorset-ancestors.com/?p=694

Chapter 21

Adams, Jad *Women and the Vote: A World History* Oxford University Press (2016)

Alberti, Johanna *Beyond Suffrage: Feminists in War and Peace 1914–28* Macmillan (1989)

Andrews, Maggie and Lomas, Janis *101 Things you Need to Know about Suffragettes* The History Press (2018)

Crawford, Elizabeth *The Women's Suffrage Movement: A Reference Guide 1866–1928* Routledge (2000)

Harrison, Brian *Separate Spheres: The Opposition to Women's Suffrage in Britain* Routledge (2012)

Holton, Sandra Stanley *Feminism and Democracy: Women's Suffrage and Reform Politics in Britain 1900–1918* Cambridge University Press (1986)

Holton, Sandra Stanley *Quaker Women: Personal Life, Memory and Radicalism in The Lives of Women Friends 1780–1930* Routledge (2007)

Holton, Sandra Stanley *Suffrage Days: Stories from The Women's Suffrage Movement* Routledge (2002)

Kent, Susan Kingsley *Sex and Suffrage in Britain 1860–1914* Routledge (1990)

King, Steven *Women, Welfare and Local Politics, 1880–1920: 'We Might be Trusted'* Sussex Academic Press (2006)

Law, Cheryl *Suffrage and Power: The Women's Movement 1918–1928* I.B. Tauris (1997)

Liddington, Jill *Rebel Girls: Their Fight for the Vote* Virago (2008)

Liddington, Jill *Vanishing for the Vote: Suffrage, Citizenship and the Battle for the Census* Manchester University Press (2014)

Marlow, Joyce *Suffragettes: The Fight for Votes for Women* Virago (2015)

Pankhurst, E. Sylvia *The Suffragette Movement: An Intimate Account of Persons and Ideals* Wharton Press (2010)

Pugh, Martin *Women and the Women's Movement in Britain 1914–1959* Marlowe & Co. (1995)

Robinson, Jane *Hearts and Minds: The Untold Story of The Great Pilgrimage and How Women Won the Vote* Doubleday (2018)

Rosen, Andrew *Rise up, Women!: The Militant Campaign of the Women's Social and Political Union, 1903–1914* Routledge (2012)

Ryan, Louise and Ward, Margaret *Irish Women and the Vote: Becoming Citizens* Irish Academic Press (2007)

Watkins, Sarah-Beth *Ireland's Suffragettes* The History Press (2014)

Crawford, Elizabeth *No Vote No Census* a National Archives Podcast https://media.nationalarchives.gov.uk/index.php/no-vote-no-census/

Liddington, Jill *Vanishing for the Vote: Diverse Suffragettes Boycott the 1911 Census* a National Archives Podcast https://media.nationalarchives.gov.uk/index.php/vanishing-vote-diverse-suffragettes-boycott-1911-census/

Mapping Women's Suffrage www.mappingwomenssuffrage.org.uk

Irish Studies: Suffrage Movement in Ireland http://irishstudies.sunygeneseoenglish.org/suffrage-movement-in-ireland/

TNA (London): Research Guide to Women's Suffrage www.nationalarchives.gov.uk/help-with-your-research/research-guides/womens-suffrage/

London School of Economics Women's Suffrage Collections www.lse.ac.uk/library/collection-highlights/womens-suffrage

Parliament UK: Women and the Vote www.parliament.uk/about/living-heritage/transformingsociety/electionsvoting/womenvote/

100 Women: Suffragists or suffragettes – who won women the vote? www.bbc.co.uk/news/world-42879161

Woman and her Sphere: Suffrage Stories https://womanandhersphere.com/suffrage-stories/

Chapter 22

Balmuth, Miriam 'Female Education in 16th and 17th Century England' in *Canadian Women's Studies* (1988) Vol. 9 nos. 3 & 4 pp.17–20

Chapman, Colin *The Growth of British Education and its Records* Lochin Publishing (1991)

Horn, Pamela *The Victorian and Edwardian Schoolchild* Alan Sutton (1989)

Lofting, Morgan 'Dangerous Minds: a perspective on women's education in Tudor/Stuart England' in *UCLA Historical Journal* 17 (1997) pp.20–58

Rich, R.W. *The Training of Teachers in England And Wales During the Nineteenth Century* Cambridge University Press (1933)

Robinson, Wendy 'Teacher Training in England and Wales: past, present and future perspectives' in *Education Research and Perspectives* Vol. 33.2 (2006) pp.19–36

Robinson, Wendy 'Women and Teacher Training: women and pupil-teacher centres, 1880–1914' in Goodman, J. and Harrop, S. (eds.) *Authoritative Women: Women, Educational Policy Making and Administration in England 1800–1954* Routledge (2000) pp.99–115

Robinson, Wendy *Pupil Teachers and their Professional Training in Pupil-Teacher Centres in England and Wales 1870–1914* Edwin Mellen Press Limited (2003)

Stephens, W.B. and Unwin, R.W. *Materials for The Local and Regional Study of Schooling 1700–1900* British Records Association (1987)

Chapter 23

Goodby, Miranda *Working Conditions in the 19th-century Staffordshire Potteries* Gardiner Signature Lecture Series (2022) www.youtube.com/watch?v=lB6-HqJajAs&ab_channel=GardinerMuseum

Jones, Mervyn *Potbank* Martin Seeker and Warsburg (1961)

McFarland, Joan 'Pottery Industry: a case of lost potential' in *Atlantis* Vol. 1.1 (Autumn 1985) pp.23–38 https://core.ac.uk/download/pdf/322499066.pdf

Sarsby, Jacqueline *Missuses and Mouldrunners: An Oral History of Women Pottery Workers at Work and at Home* Oxford University Press (1988)

Scriven, Samuel *Her Majesties Commissioners on the Employment of Children and Young Persons in the District of the Staffordshire Potteries and on the Actual State, Condition and Treatment of such Children and Young Persons* HMSO (1841). The full text is available at www.thepotteries.org/history/scriven.htm

Sekers, David *The Potteries* Shire Publications (1981)

The Potteries.org www.thepotteries.org
The Minton Archive www.themintonarchive.org.uk

Index

Abortion, 15
Age of consent, 32, 37
Aitchison, Helen, 93–4
Aitchison, William Douglas, 93–4
Amalgamated Society of Glovers, 65
Anthony, Susan B., 125
Army Nursing Service, *see* Queen Alexandra's Royal Army Nursing Corps
Arrowsmith, Mr T., 141
Aston Clinton, Buckinghamshire, 16, 19–21
Aston, John, 122
Aylesbury, Buckinghamshire, 21

Baker, Ann, 140
Baking, 59, 61, 73, 80, 111
Balfour, Lord, 135
Barber Surgeons' Guild, 90
Barnbow Munitions Factory, 7–8
Barry, James, 55
Barry, Miranda, 55
Battledore, *see* laundry bat
Beale, Dorothea, 134
Beeken, Ellen, 93
Beetle, *see* laundry bat
Beeton, Isabella, 11, 13, 49, 79
Benley, William, 139

Berney, Blanche Marguerite, 41
Berney, Cyril, 1
Berney, Henri, 40–3
Berney, Leonard, 44
Berney, Reginald, 42–3
Besant, Annie, 24–5
Bird's Eyes, 121
Blackford, Blanche Marguerite, 41
Blackford, Cyril, 41
Blackford, Hannah, 40
Blackford, Margaret, 39–44
Blackford, Mark, 40
Blackford, Phyllis, 43–4
Blackford, Reginald, 42–3
Blackwell, Elizabeth, 55
Bladford Cartwheels, 121
Blakely's Mill, 116
Bleaching, 3, 109
Blue Stockings Society, 131
Bobbin lace, 83–4
Bodichon, Barbara, 133
Bon Marche, 100
Bourne and Hollingsworth, 40
Bowden, G.F., 145
Box mangles, 109
Brain, Mr E., 142
British and Foreign Schools, 133
British Medical Association, 56

British Medical Journal, 57
British Nurses' Association, 52
British Nursing Association, 52
British Penitent Female Refuge, The, 39
Bryant and May, 23–6
Bryant, Frederick, 25
Bryant, William, 23
Buckingham, Elizabeth, 38
Buckingham, Philip, 38
Bucking-tubs, 109
Burmantofts Pottery, 141
Burslem, Staffordshire, 145–6
Buss, Frances, 133
Butler, Josephine, 37
Butter churns, 74
Butter, 73–5
Button Day, 121
Byssinosis, 114

Carding, 2
Case, Abraham, 120
Case, Peter, 121
Castlemaine, Lady, 31
Cat and Mouse' Act, 128
Caton, Harriet, 145–146
Caton, Joseph, 145–148
Caton, Lavinia, 147
Caton, Thomas Joseph, 146
Caton, William, 146
Caton, Wilmot, 146
Cattern cakes, 85
Ceasarion section, 87
Central Midwives Board, 89, 96

Central Register for Civilian Nurses, 53
Chamberlen, Peter, 90
Cheese, 74–6
Cheltenham Ladies' College, 134
Childbed fever, 86
Children's Employment Commission, 14, 23, 85, 141
Civil Rights Movement, 125
Clean Air Acts, 77
Clifford, Rosamund, 31
Clotworthue, Catherine, 38
Contagious Diseases Acts, 36–7
Contraception, 87
Cooks, 10–11
Cotton Famine, 114
Cousins, Margaret, 126
Crimean War, 51
Crompton's Mule, 113
Cross Commission, 135
Culpeper, Nicholas, 46

Dairies, 72
Dame schools, 132
Daniel, Mr, 139
Dartmoor Prison, 144
Davidson, Emily, 128
Davies, Emily, 133
Death's Head, 122
Dickens, Charles, 39
Dishley, Ann, 140
Dolben, Sir William, 33
Dorset Knobs, 120
Dr Williams' Little Pink Pills, 49

Drinks, 62–3
Dublin Women's Suffrage
    Association, 126
Dying, 2

Early Closing Association, 100
Education Act 1902, 135
Elizabeth I, 131
Embroidery, 4, 82
English Woman's Domestic
    Magazine, 49, 78

Factory Act 1833, 113
Factory Act 1847, 113
Factory Acts, 85, 113
Factory and Workshop Regulation
    Act, 18
Fenians, 25
Fenwick, Ethel, 52
Fieldhouse, Ada, 117–19
Fieldhouse, Annie, 119
Fieldhouse, Ernest, 119
Fieldhouse, James, 117
First World War, 6, 56, 102–03
Fish-curing, 28–29
French Hospital, 42
Fry, Elizabeth, 53
Fry, Henry Davidson, 91
Fuel, 59–60
Fuller's earth, 109

Garrett Anderson, Elizabeth, 55–6
General Medical Council, 55
General Nursing Council, 9
Gerard, John, 46, 48

Germ theory, 87
Girls' Friendly Society, 13
Girls' Day School Trust, 134
Girton College, 133
Gladstone, William, 39
Glove Tax, 65
Glove-making areas, 65
Gloving donkeys, 66
Goodsell family, 42
Gordon, Dr Alexander, 86
Governesses' Benevolent Institution,
    132
Great Exhibition, 120
Great Kimble, Buckinghamshire,
    21–2
Greenhow, Dr, 138
Grene, John, 38
Grey, Hilda, 92
Grey, Maria, 134
Guard, Annie, 69
Guard, Archibald, 70
Guard, Beatrice May, 70
Guard, Lilian Norah, 68–71
Guard, Mary, 68–70
Guard, Philip, 69
Gurney, Mary, 134
Guy's Hospital, 52
Gwynn, Nell, 31

Hairdressing, 11
Hanley, Staffordshire, 143–6
Harbord, Sidney, 40, 43
Harris' List of Covent Garden
    Ladies, 35
Haslam, Anna, 126

Hazlitt, William, 75
Henderson, Mrs, 92
Herbert, Sidney, 52
High Tops, 122
Holt, Harold Edward Sherwin, 95
Home Rule, 126
Honeycomb Crosswheels, 121
Hooley Hill Rubber and Chemical Works, 8
Hospital Records' Database, 52
Housekeepers, 11
Housemaids, 11
Howe, Mary Ann, 21
Howe, William, 21–2
Humanist Movement, 131

Infant mortality, 89
Inquiries Concerning Female Labour in the Metropolis, 14, 28
Irish Women's Franchise League, 126
Ironing, 110–11
Irvine, Robert Henry Lairde, 95

Jack the Ripper, 37
Jacquard, 113
Jex Blake, Sophia, 56

Kay's Flying Shuttle, 113
Kelly, Mary, 68–70
Kingham, Grace, 19–20
Kings College Hospital, 56
Kitchen maids, 12
Knitting, 3
Knox, John, 131

Labour-saving devices, 10, 77, 81, 106
Lace making schools, 84
Lady's maids, 11
Langham Place Group, 98
Langtry, Lily, 31
Laundries, 112
Laundry bat, 107
Le Cour, James, 89
Leek Buttons, 122
Leghorn, Italy, 15
Lister, Joseph, 87
Lloyd George, David, 6
Lock Hospitals, 37
London School of Medicine for Women, 56
London Society for the Prootection of Young Females, 36
Long, Dr, 92
Longe, Francis, 141
Luther, Martin, 131
Luton, Bedfordshire, 16, 20
Lye, 108–109
Lying-in hospitals, 86

Macaulay, Lord, 133
Magdalen Hospital for the Reception of Penitant Prostitutes, 39
Magdalene Laundries, 39
Maid-of-all-work, 13
Majolica ware, 142
Mangles, 110
Markham, Gervase, 72–3, 75, 88
Marriage bar, 16, 97, 135
Married Women's Property Act, 147
Matrimonial Causes Act, 147

May, Francis, 23
Mayhew, Henry, 31–2, 35–6, 116
McClung, Nellie, 125
Mechanics' Institute, 133
Medical Act, 1876, 56
Medical Directories, 56–7
Medical Registers, 56
Meigh, Charles and sons, 144
Meigs, Dr Charles, 86–7
Metropolitan Association for Befriending Young Servants, 13
Midwives Act, 1902, 89
Midwives Roll, 95
Mill, John Stuart, 127
Milliner, Mrs, 148
Ministry of Agriculture and Fisheries, 103
Mitres, 121
Monitorial system, 133
Montagu, Elizabeth, 131
Morecombe Winter Gardens, 119
Mottershead family, 123
Mulcaster, Richard, 131

National Council of Nurses of Great Britain and Ireland, 52
National Schools, 133
National Shell Filling Factory, 8
National Union of Glovers, 65, 67
National Union of Women's Suffrage Societies, 127
National Vigilance Association, The, 14
National Women's Party, 125
Newfoundland, 27

Nightingale, Florence, 51–2
North London Collegiate School for Ladies, 134
North Staffordshire Chamber of Commerce, 142
Nurses' Registration Act, 52

Offal, 61–2
Ogden, Marian, 141

Palmer, Charles, 95
Palmer, Emily, 95
Pankhurst, Christobel, 128
Pankhurst, Edna, 143–4
Pankhurst, Emmeline, 125, 127, 143
Pankhurst, Francis, 147–8
Pankhurst, Harriet, 145–6
Pankhurst, Henry, 146
Pankhurst, Mary, 143–8
Pankhurst, Thomas Joseph Caton, 146
Pankhurst, William Horatio, 143–4
Parlour maids, 12, 14
Passementerie Buttons, 122
Pasteur, Louis, 87
Paul, Alice, 125
Penance, 38
Pennington, William, 146
Pentonville Prison, 43
Pepys, Samuel, 15, 75
Pillow lace, 83–4
Pitt, William the younger, 65
Plait schools, 17–18
Political Equality League, 125
Poor Law Amendment Act, 20
Portland Prison, 43

Postmistresses, 97
Potteries, Trades and Labour Council, 142
Pre-eclampsia, 87
Preserving food, 60–1
Prisoners' Temporary Discharge for Ill-health Act, 128
Puerperal pyrexia, 86, 92
Pupil teachers, 135

Queen Alexandra's Royal Army Nursing Corps, 54
Queen Alexandra's Imperial Military Nursing Service, *see* Queen Alexandra's Royal Army Nursing Corps
Queen's College, London, 132
Queen's Nursing Institute, 53

Rag-sorting, 115–116
Rake, Charles Patrick, 94
Rake, Edward Archibald, 94
Rake, Edward, 94
Rake, Ethel Margaret, 94
Rake, Mary, 92–6
Rake, Talbot Eustace, 94
Rake, Violet, 94–96
Reckitt's Blue, 107
Reformation, 131
Rennet, 75
Ridgeway, 140
Robinson, Mrs, 42–3
Roedean School, 134
Row, Charles, 123
Royal College of Nursing, 53

Royal College of Obstetricians and Gynaecologists, 89
Royal College of Obstetricians and Gynaecologists, 89
Royal Commission on the Employment of Children, Young Persons and Women in Agriculture, 19
Royal Doulton, 137
Royal Free Hospital, 56
Royal Greenwich Hospital, 55
Royal Maternity Charity for Delivering Poor Married women, 89
Royal Maternity Charity, 89, 93
Ryan, Doctor, 35

Salt, Sir Titus, 117–18
Saltaire Congregational Church, 118
Saltaire, 117
Salvation Army, 26, 70
Saunders, Benjamin, 122
Saunderton Workhouse Infirmary, 22
Scriven, Samuel, 138–141
Scullery maids, 12
Seacole, Mary, 51
Seats for Shop Assistants Act, 100
Second World War, 6–7, 50, 103–105
Semmelweis, Ignaz, 86
Sex Disqualification Removal Act of 1919, 135
Sharpe, Jane, 88
Sheehy-Skeffington, Francis, 126
Sheehy-Skeffington, Hannah, 126
Shell crisis, 6
Shepherd, Mary Ann, 117

Sheppard, Kate, 124
Shirreff, Emily, 134
Shop Act, 101
Shop Assistants' Union, 100
Shop Hours Acts, 100
Shop, Distributive and Allied Workers Union, 100
Short, Ethel Florence, 136
Silvertown Munitions Factory, 6
Sleech, John, 38
Social Democratic Foundation, 25
Society for the State Registration of Nurses, 52
Spaeth, Louis, 91–2
Spangles, 121
Spin-dryers, 108
Spinning Jenny, 113
Spinning, 4
Spring cleaning, 80–81
St Hilda's College, 134
Stanley, Lady, 134
Stanton, Elizabeth Cady, 125
Starch, 110
State Enrolled Nurses, 53
State Registered Nurses, 53
Stead, William Thomas, 37
Stone, Lucy, 125
Stratford, Ann, 16, 19–22
Stratford, Henry, 16
Stratford, Peter, 16
Stratford, Richard, 16, 19
Straw splitting, 17
Suffrage petitions, 125–7
Suffragette, The, 128
Suffragettes, 124–8

Suffragists, 124–9
Swell's Night Guide to the Bowers of Venus, 35
Swing Riots, 20
Sykes, Dr, 93

Talbot, Dame Meriel, 102
Teacher Training Colleges, 134–5
Teachers' Registration Council, 136
Ten-spoke Yarrels, 121
Territorial Force Nursing Service, 54
Thackrah, Charles, 115
Thorn, Mr, 21
Toxemia, 87
Tring, Hertfordshire, 21
Truck Act, 99
Tunstall, Staffordshire, 145
Turner, Edith, 70
Turner, Eva, 71
Turner, Henry, 71
Turner, John Henry, 70
Turner, John, 70

Union of Women Match Makers, 26
United Glovers Mutual Aid Society, 65
Urania Cottage, 39

Vagrancy Act, 36
Vaughan Tapscott, 70–71
Vesey, Elizabeth, 131
Victoriana, 42
Voluntary Aid Detachment (VAD), 55, 95

Wade, Charles, 94
Wade, Mary Ann, 92
Wages, 10, 20, 29, 99
Walsh, Mrs, 145
Washing machines, 109
Washing powder, 108
Washing-up, 80
Water collecting, 106–107
Weaving, 4
Wedgwood, 137
Wellcome Library, 53, 57
Wesley, John, 49
Wet nurses, 55, 90
Whitely, William, 99
Wilberforce, William, 36
Withington, Lancashire, 143

Women's Christian Temperance Union, 124, 126
Women's Social and Political Union, 124, 127
Women's Christian Temperance Union, 124–6
Women's National Land Service Corps, 102
Women's Timber Corps, 105
Wood, Fanny, 139
Woodward, Mrs, 42
Woolley, Hannah, 12, 46–7, 74, 90
Worrelow, Mary, 140
Worshipful Society of Apothecaries, 56
Wrench, Mrs, 146